About us . . .

These walks were written and mapped by Diana and Peter Gulland of Haddenham, who also devised the routes, except for that of the Aylesbury Ring (Walk 16). The idea of the Ring was conceived and developed by Ray Knowles and John Maples of Aylesbury. When the route descriptions were complete, they were tried out on the paths by Tom Berry, Hugh Granger, Ray Knowles, and Ken and Sibyl Rhead. All the checkers returned to tell their tales, and to suggest improvements, which have been incorporated into the text. If, however, any ambiguities or mistakes remain, the responsibility lies with Diana and Peter.

. . . and the book . . .

"The Vale of Aylesbury Walker" replaces the Ramblers' Association's previous book of walks in the area entitled "On Foot in the Vale of Aylesbury", published in 1978. It was when "On Foot" became out of print that we considered whether to simply republish it with its route descriptions brought up to date, or to start afresh. The outcome was that three walks from "On Foot" have been updated and carried forward into the present book, as walks 4, 10 and 14. The remainder of the walks are either completely new, or are such extensive revisions of the routes of "On Foot" walks that they amount to new walks.

. . . and the Ramblers' Association

Most of the people involved in writing and checking this book are members of the Ramblers' Association, the national organisation which represents everyone who enjoys a walk in the country. Much of the Association's work is carried out by unpaid volunteers. On the one hand its many local groups organise rambles most weekends. On the other hand some members help to keep the paths open by clearing away overgrowth and building stiles and simple footbridges. Members alert highway authorities when paths are illegally obstructed and the Association is consulted on formal proposals to divert or extinguish them. At national level the Association plays a major role in gaining and improving legislation which protects your footpath heritage.

If you join us you would be put in touch with your local group's activities as well as receiving a national magazine which would keep you up to date on issues affecting footpaths. You would also be adding your weight to the Association's voice.

Please write for further details to: Ramblers' Association, Headquarters, 1/5, Wandsworth Road, London SW8 2XX.

The Walks

Getting ready to go

Food

The walks in this book take you to parts of the Vale which are off the beaten track. Consequently you will find eating and drinking places a little thin on the ground. Where there are pubs and grocers on the route they are mentioned at the beginning of each walk. However, you will see that some walks don't pass many of them; it is advisable to take a little something with you to eat and drink.

Footwear

There is a lot of clay in the lower-lying parts of the Vale of Aylesbury. This holds water well so that, after prolonged rain in winter, some very muddy patches and local minor flooding can occur. Our advice for such times is to wear wellington boots. For the rest of the year, stout walking shoes or boots will give the protection you need.

Maps

Our intention is that our route descriptions, read with our sketch maps, are sufficiently detailed for you to find your way without the need for other maps. If, however, you want to look at the landscape you are walking through in more detail, please read on.

All the walks in this book lie within the area covered by the Ordnance Survey "Landranger" (1:50,000 scale) map no. 165. However, while this is useful for finding the start of your walk, and for generally setting the scene, it is not detailed enough to enable you to follow the twists and turns of footpaths with any accuracy. We recommend that, if you want to use a map, you bring an Ordnance Survey 1:25,000 scale "Pathfinder" map. The numbers of the relevant sheets are given at the head of each walk.

Take a watch

Most of our walks are well-provided with barns, field corners, gates, church towers etc. which act as suitable landmarks for walkers to aim at. Every now and then we are without any of these and resort to giving directions by reference to a clock face. At such times we assume that the clock is aligned with the 12 o'clock–6 o'clock axis at a right angle to the hedge or fence you have just come through, and we tell you to aim at 10 o'clock, or 1 o'clock etc. The difference between, e.g., 10 o'clock and 11 o'clock can be quite considerable when projected across a large field so *please wear a watch with a dial*; in tests without watches we have found that some people have a remarkably vague idea of precisely what direction is implied by, e.g., 10 o'clock!

Getting there by public transport

Most of the walks in this book are easily reached by public transport; indeed, this is the best way of getting to and from various sections of walks 9, 15 and 16.

The approximate frequency of the relevant bus and train services is given at the start of each walk. You are strongly recommended to check with individual operators for actual times before setting out. The relevant contacts for the principal bus services are:

Aylesbury Bus, Enquiry Office, Aylesbury Bus Station (telephone: Aylesbury (0296) 84919)

Bee Line, Travel Office, High Wycombe Bus Station (telephone: High Wycombe (0494) 20941)

London Country North West, Hemel Hempstead Garage (telephone: Hemel Hempstead (0442) 55619)

Oxford Bus, 395, Cowley Road, Oxford (telephone: Oxford (0865) 711312)

Red Rover, see *Aylesbury Bus*

If you have difficulty in obtaining travel information, Bucks County Council's "Bus Line" enquiry service is available during Monday to Friday office hours on Aylesbury (0296) 382000.

Once you are walking

Finding your way

A number of the paths in this book are quite lightly used. In consequence they are not always visible on the ground but this must not deter you from following the route described. During the growing season the footprints of the last walker on the path can quickly be obscured and for this reason we give the routes in some detail. Please remember that the route described is the legal line of path. Our purpose in writing this book is to enable you to enjoy your legal right of way without trespassing on the private land through which that way passes.

If the path is obstructed

At the time of their selection for this book, the paths used were generally unobstructed. The few obstructions found are usually noted in the text and have been put in hand for attention. However, the state of paths in the countryside is constantly changing, and new obstructions may appear, some thoughtlessly, and some through wear and tear. If you find your walk hindered by, for example, a missing or damaged footbridge, an impassable hedge or fence, or a midfield path with a crop growing on it, please report the matter (with careful details of location, including a grid reference) to:

The County Engineer,		The Footpath Officer,
Bucks County Council,*	*or*	Aylesbury Vale District Council,**
County Hall,		The Mall,
Aylesbury HP20 1UY		Friars Square,
		Aylesbury HP20 2SR

*Except for walk 15 from Wheatley to Ickford Bridge (which is in Oxfordshire), and for walk 16's section between a bridge south of Hulcott to near Puttenham Lock (which is in Hertfordshire).
**Except for the whole of walk 13, walk 15 from Wheatley to Ickford Bridge, and walk 16 from a bridge south of Hulcott to near Puttenham Lock, and from Wellwick Farm, Wendover to Kimble Wick.

KEY TO THE MAPS

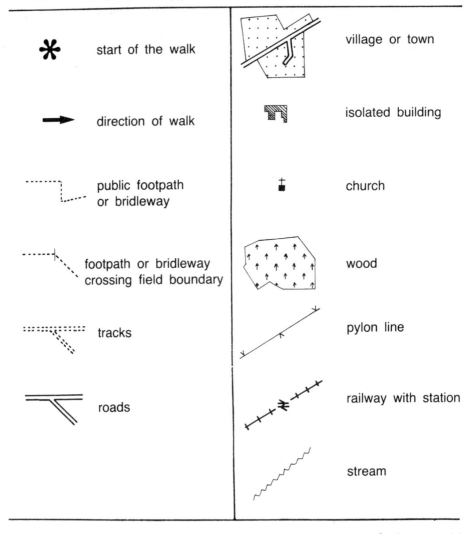

✱ start of the walk	village or town
→ direction of walk	isolated building
public footpath or bridleway	church
footpath or bridleway crossing field boundary	wood
tracks	pylon line
roads	railway with station
	stream

All maps in this book are based on the Ordnance Survey 1:25,000 scale maps with the permission of the Controller of Her Majesty's Stationery Office. © Crown Copyright.

Tom Stephenson's Walk

Walk 1	2 miles
O.S. 1:25,000 scale map SP71 (Pathfinder Series 1093)	

CUDDINGTON — NETHER WINCHENDON — CUDDINGTON

Starting point: Cuddington Village Green (Grid ref: 738111)

Cuddington is an appropriate place in which to start this series of walks for here Tom Stephenson lived from 1962 until his death. Tom (1893–1987) pioneered The Pennine Way, Britain's first Long Distance Footpath, and for many years was National Secretary of The Ramblers' Association; he was one of Britain's most eminent ramblers. In Cuddington he lived in a bungalow with panoramic views across the beautiful valley of the River Thame and often walked the local paths until declining health prevented this.

Travel

Motorists will usually find room to park considerately in Upper Church Street, which runs downhill from the village green on the Aylesbury–Chearsley road.

Bus users can alight at Cuddington village green from the (roughly) two-hourly weekday Oxford Bus and Aylesbury Bus joint service 260 (Aylesbury–Thame); there is no Sunday service.

Refreshments

Only in Cuddington, where there are pubs.

Route

Cuddington is a delightful, compact village which has seen little modern development. Its narrow streets are still fronted, in places, by garden walls and buildings made of witchert, the historic local building material consisting of a mixture of clay, chopped straw, and stones.

The fine Elizabethan house standing across the road from the parish church is Tyringham Hall. It was built in the early seventeenth century to be the home of the Tyringham family, who acquired the Manor of Cuddington in the sixteenth century.

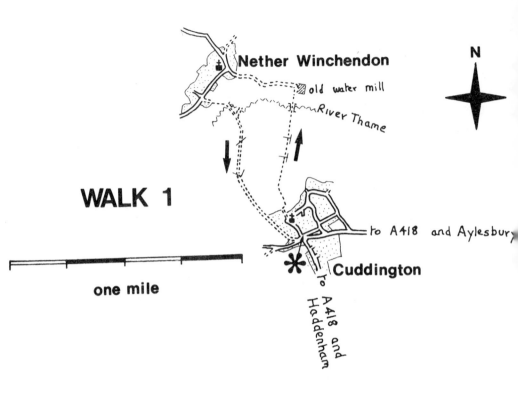

Start at the village green and set off down Upper Church Street, soon to pass the parish church on your right. Immediately after the street has swung sharp right behind the church, turn left down Tibbys Lane, which runs down the side of Tyringham Hall. At the end of the lane bear right on to a footpath (metalled at first) which skirts Tibby's Cottage and its garden. When the path forks, bear left to cross a footbridge over a small man-made waterfall.

Once across the bridge follow the right-hand side of the field as it curves and drops away into the valley ahead. In the bottom right-hand corner of the field climb the stile ahead and continue in the same direction (now on the valley bottom) along the right-hand side of two more fields to reach and cross the footbridge over the River Thame. On again along the right-hand side of one more field to join the gravelled drive in front of the house which was once part of Nether Winchendon Mill.

> **The water mill itself stood at the Cuddington end of the building prior to demolition and some of its working parts were lying on the ground in front of it until the 1970's. The mill stream has been filled in above the mill (on your right) but survives, slowly silting up, on your left.**

Turn left along the farm track at the far end of the mill buildings and follow it into the picturesque village of Nether Winchendon.

As you enter the village you skirt the grounds of Nether Winchendon House on your left. The house is essentially of fifteenth-century origin, and was heavily Gothicised in 1797–1803, as is evident when you pause to view it from its gateway. It has been the home of the Spencer-Bernard family for over 400 years, before which it was in the hands of the Augustinian monks at nearby Notley Abbey. Please turn to page 98 for notes on the village.

On reaching the small village green (note the unusual one-handed clock on the church tower) bear left along the road and soon pass the former village school (closed 1975, now a dwelling) and the unusually large farmhouse at Manor Farm. Three hundred yards beyond the church turn left off the road on to an access track which starts opposite a public telephone box. After some 50 yards the track passes close by the end of a timber-framed cottage, and continues ahead as a concrete footpath between fences.

A footbridge takes the path over the River Thame. On reaching the southern bank continue ahead on a causeway raised slightly above the Thame's flood plain. The causeway is soon joined by a private drive which comes in on the left from Nether Winchendon House. Your route is ahead on an easily-followed access track for the next ⅔ mile, first on the causeway, then curving left and climbing between fields to return to the village green at Cuddington.

The group of bungalows passed on the left as you re-enter the village is an interesting 1980's development of barns in a former farmyard. Just before reaching the green you pass a gatehouse with over-sailing first floor. In case it gives you that "I've been here before" feeling it is worth mentioning that it is a (relatively) modern copy of the old school at Whitchurch, north of Aylesbury.

Chinkwell Wood

Walk 2	2¼ miles
O.S. 1:25,000 scale map SP61 (Pathfinder Series 1093)	

BRILL — CHINKWELL WOOD — BRILL

Starting point: Brill Parish Church (Grid ref: 656138)

Although this is a short walk, it takes you through widely contrasting surroundings. As you leave the hilltop village of Brill a magnificent panorama across north Buckinghamshire takes your attention. However, after reaching the foot of the hill, a walk through Chinkwell Wood cuts off all views of the outside world and sounds become dominated by the wind in the trees and the songs of woodland birds. Waterproof footwear is advised to combat a couple of small but wet areas on the outward section.

Travel

See introduction to walk no. 12.

Refreshments

Brill has grocery shops in High Street and Temple Street and also several pubs. There are no other refreshment opportunities on this walk.

Route

Start at the churchyard gate at the west (tower) end of the parish church. Set off along the fenced track which passes the west side of the churchyard (thereby leaving the church on your right) to reach the village's playing field.

On entering the playing field the track cuts through part of the Civil War earth rampart which was dug along the outside of this part of the village. It is best seen over the fence on your left.

Pass to the left of the brick-built pavilion and continue straight ahead along the left-hand side of the playing field. On crossing a concrete path to the school change direction to bear diagonally right across the remainder of the playing field. This brings you to the gate and stile seen in the fence ahead at the left-hand corner of the school grounds. Climb the stile and maintain the same course across the top corner of the field beyond. Do not go through the

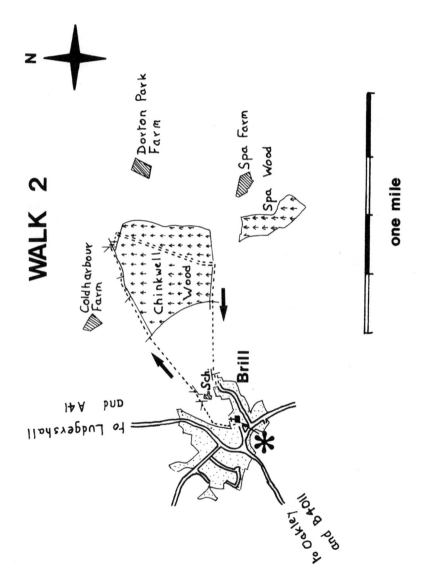

WALK 2

N

Dorton Park
Farm

Coldharbour
Farm

Chinkwell
Wood

Spa Farm

Spa Wood

Sch.

Brill

To Ludgershall
and A41

To Oakley
and B4011

one mile

11

gateway in the hedge in front of you but climb the stile into the field corner immediately on its left. Now, with much of North Buckinghamshire spread out before you, set off downhill beside the hedge/fence on the right. In the bottom right-hand corner of the field cross the fence ahead and continue in the same direction (now with Chinkwell Wood on the right) along the right-hand side of three more fields. On reaching the far right-hand corner of the third field (and the end of the wood) go straight ahead through the gate in front of you in the corner, turn right along the farm track behind it, and immediately go through another gate. Walk towards the wood for 15 yards, then turn left through a third gate into a field and set off downhill beside the edge of the wood on your right.

Ahead of you in the valley the village of Dorton can be seen, with the buildings of Dorton Park Farm situated half-way between you and the village.

After 100 yards turn right from the field into a straight woodland ride and follow it for nearly ½ mile across Chinkwell Wood.

On reaching the other side of the wood, cross the footbridge and stile into a large sloping field. Turn right and walk uphill along the right-hand side of the field, following the edge of the wood. At the top corner of the field (and the wood) go through the small gate in the fence ahead and continue uphill beside the fence on your right.

The two lines of new trees, interspersed with the stumps of old ones, mark the site of the grand avenue from Brill down to the one-time Dorton Spa (in the wood behind you on your left). See page 70 for details of the Spa.

Go through the gate in the top right-hand corner of the field and ahead on the unmade track along the edge of a housing estate. This brings you on to a residential road in Brill. Follow it back to the green.

The Wotton Estate

CIRCULAR WALK FROM WOTTON UNDERWOOD IN THE GENERAL DIRECTION OF KINGSWOOD AND WESTCOTT

Starting point: Wotton Underwood Church (Grid ref: 688159)

The walks in this book visit some villages in which, almost unbelievably in this age of change, time really seems to have stood still. Wotton Underwood is one such place, a tiny hamlet steeped in the history of England through the fortunes of the Grenville family. They were Lords of the Manor here from the fourteenth to the nineteenth century and their fortunes accelerated in the seventeenth century following a marriage to the Temple family of Stowe. By the late eighteenth century the senior descendant of the Grenville family was living at Stowe with the title of Earl Temple, and in 1822 he was created Duke of Buckingham and Chandos. Although the family had thus moved their main place of residence to Stowe, Wotton remained the ancestral home, and it was to Wotton that many were brought to be buried.

Wotton House, home of the Grenvilles, once stood in extensive parkland, and over half of the walk is through countryside which was once part of that park. Today the parkland has shrunk to an area on the west side of the House, to which there is no public access. As you follow this walk the only clues to the historic parkland landscape that it crosses are the unusual scattering of estate cottages, and one or two isolated landscape features which were once part of the Park.

Travel

The nearby bus service is too sparse to be of use in reaching this walk. Motorists will find a small parking area (2–3 cars) in front of Wotton Underwood church. If this is full, please drive back ¼ mile (round two corners) to park on the broad verges of the long straight section of road leading away from Wotton. Please do not park on the village green (not even two wheels).

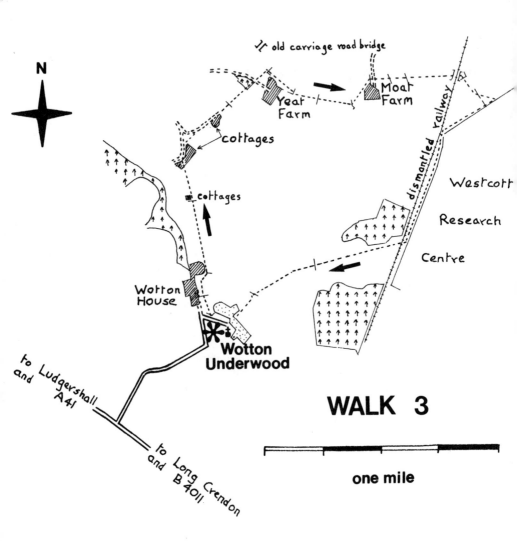

old carriage road bridge

Yeat Farm

Moat Farm

cottages

cottages

Westcott

Research

Centre

dismantled railway

Wotton House

Wotton Underwood

to Ludgershall and A41

to Long Crendon and B4011

WALK 3

one mile

N

14

Refreshments

There are no shops or pubs on this circuit.

Route

All Saints Church, Wotton, is perhaps most noteworthy for the family chapel of the Dukes of Buckingham and Chandos. Here lie three Dukes of Buckingham, two Prime Ministers, a First Lord of the Admiralty, a Secretary of State for Ireland, and a Governor of Madras in some of the 26 family tombs which crowd the chapel, 18 of them in an unusual double-decked arrangement. Such a lot of English history in such a secluded corner of England.

With your back to the churchyard gates set off back along the narrow road. After 130 yards (just after the access track to the farmhouse on right) turn right on to a concrete footpath which quickly goes through a kissing gate. Follow this path uphill, through another gate, and past the frontage of Wotton House.

Wotton House, with its two flanking pavilions, was built in 1704–1714 for the Grenville family. It is now hard to believe that by 1950 it stood ruinous, awaiting demolition. Almost by chance Mrs P. Brunner, the owner of a historic building in the south of the county, was brought to Wotton in search of items to salvage for use in the garden of her house. She had never seen Wotton House before but she fell in love with it, bought it, and carried out a painstaking restoration so that today it is back in residential use (now as flats).

Stay on the concrete path as it runs on across fields. After a while you pass a pair of estate cottages on the left (note "B&C 1887" on the gable ends, referring to the Dukes of Buckingham & Chandos). Two hundred and fifty yards further on the path passes between two more pairs of cottages, then converges with an unmade access track and continues ahead beside it.

Note the dramatic modern glass-walled house set back from the path on right. Just after the unmade track diverges to the left, the concrete path comes to an end against another unmade track. Bear slightly to right to maintain your course, now on the latter track. Stay on this track when, 100 yards further on, it bends to right and goes through a gateway. Two more isolated houses are passed on right, and the track ends by turning into the garden of the second of them. When it does this, maintain your course ahead, now on a grass footpath (fenced at first) which runs beside the hedge along the right-hand side of two fields.

Over the hedge on your right you will notice a pattern of indistinct low earthworks, including two partly silted up ponds, in the grass. These are some of the remains of the village of Wotton which was cleared away in the eighteenth century to make room for the landscaped park around Wotton House.

In the corner at the end of the second field (with houses now close ahead), go through the gate ahead. Maintain the same course along the edge of a copse beside a stable block and house to go through a pedestrian gate on to a farm road. Cross over the road, go through the gate opposite, and ahead in the field to pass the side of the house on right.

The isolated road bridge seen ahead on left is part of the original carriage road from Wotton House to the London road at Kingswood. The fine avenue of trees seen half a mile beyond it once flanked this carriage road.

Turn right through the gate immediately behind the house, follow the boundary along the back of that house and the side of the adjoining farm (Yeat Farm), then continue straight ahead across the field to go over the stile facing you in the right-hand corner ahead. From the stile (with Yeat Farm now behind you) go straight ahead across the next two fields, aiming for the top of the tree-clad Lodge Hill in the first field and slightly to left of it in the second. Pass through a wide gap in the hedge between these fields; go through a small gate in the hedge on the far side of the second field. Once through this gate ignore the gate facing you 100 yards ahead and bear left across the field to join and walk beside the boundary of Moat Farm on your *right*.

In the grounds of the farm house notice the remaining arms of the moat which once surrounded it. See page 127 for notes on moats.

This course brings you to a gate in the field corner, close to a barn. Go through the gate and, bearing *very* slightly right, cross the farm access track, go beneath the telegraph line (leave single post to left) and downhill through the gate in the hedge ahead. On, uphill, across the next field, through the gate ahead, and maintain the same course across the following field to go through the gate directly in front of the railway bridge.

This railway embankment had a relatively short life as part of the railway network. Opened to passenger traffic in 1906 as part of a bypass by which Marylebone–Sheffield/Manchester services could avoid the congested route through Harrow, Amersham and Aylesbury, it closed in 1967.

Go beneath the railway bridge and through the gate beyond into a small enclosure containing a pond. Continue through the gate to the right of the pond and on along the left-hand side of the field beyond towards the high perimeter fence and scattered buildings of the Royal Ordnance Research and Development Centre, Westcott. Ninety yards before reaching the perimeter fence, go through the gateway into the second field on the left and bear diagonally to right across the field, aiming for the wooden test tower on its artificial hill within the Westcott complex. This course brings you to the perimeter fence.

The land now inside this fence was farmland until 1940, when it was requisitioned by the RAF. Runways were laid, living quarters built, and "RAF Westcott" became a training base for Bomber Command air crews. The RAF left in 1945 and in 1946 the airfield became part of the Explosives Division of Royal Ordnance, concentrating on the testing of rocket propellants.

On reaching the perimeter fence turn right to follow it closely for ⅓ mile, crossing the several stiles beside it en route. The fence first converges on the former railway embankment, then turns left to parallel it; a kink in the fence line shortly after the left turn marks the place where a railway siding once entered Westcott. Beyond the site of the former siding a line of poplars flanks the fence; after you have followed the broad grass security strip beside these poplars for a few hundred yards you will see a windowless concrete test building sited close to the fence (perhaps 30 ft inside it). Two hundred yards beyond this test building a small plantation of young trees in the middle of the grass strip bars your way; pass to the right of it and, after a further 40 yards, turn right to drop down and cross the route of the railway.

As you cross the stile on the far side of the "railway", the distinctive shape of Wotton House appears dead ahead. Make straight towards it across the sizeable field in front of you. This course brings you down to a footbridge over the stream in front of the hedge which lies across your route (not visible until you are well into the field). Cross the bridge and stile and proceed up the following field aiming midway between Wotton House and the church to left of it, to go through a gate in the fence ahead (this gate gives access to the field immediately to the left of the one in front of Wotton House). Once through the gate, continue beside the left-hand fence as it curves towards the farm barns and go through the gate ahead into the farmyard. Skirt round the left-hand side of the barns to leave the tiny former village school on your left and return to the starting point on the village green at Wotton.

The Quainton Hills

Walk 4	4 miles

O.S. 1:25,000 scale map SP72
(Pathfinder Series 1070)

QUAINTON — QUAINTON HILL — HOGSHAW — QUAINTON

Starting point: Church Street, Quainton (Grid ref: 747201)

The hills which form a striking backdrop to the village of Quainton were common land until being enclosed in 1840. This tramp over these hills quickly brings you to panoramic views northwards from the Vale of Aylesbury into the Midland Plain.

Travel

There are no off-street parking places in Quainton. It is possible to park cars inoffensively at the church end of Church Street but it is preferable to continue past the church, down the hill, then turn right and park on the grass road verges behind the church (you can return on foot through the churchyard).

Bus users have a weekday service varying between one- and two-hourly on Red Rover routes 1 (Aylesbury–Westcott) and 15 (Aylesbury–Calvert). There is no service on Sundays.

Refreshments

Only available in Quainton, where the Village Stores are in Church Street, and pubs are scattered around the village.

Route

At the top of Quainton Green are the remains of the village cross (probably 15th-century) and behind it a house built for Judge Dormer in 1723 which bears his coat of arms. Off the route but worth a detour are the church (14th-century) and neighbouring 17th-century almshouses along Church Street. Above the Green is the recently-restored windmill, which was built around 1830. The mill was found to be in a poor location to catch the wind and in later days its main power came from a steam engine; it was the cost of moving coal to it from the nearest railway station that brought about its early abandonment.

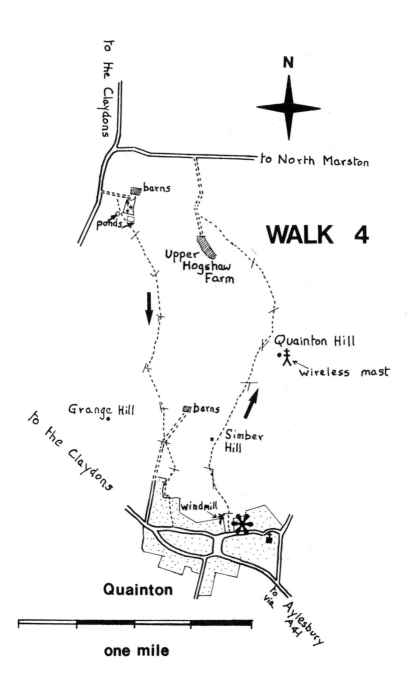

to The Claydons

N

to North Marston

barns

ponds

Upper Hogshaw Farm

WALK 4

Quainton Hill

•⊀ wireless mast

Grange Hill •

barns

Simber Hill

to the Claydons

windmill

Quainton

to Aylesbury via A41

one mile

19

The walk starts over a stile beside a gate on the north side of Church Street (opposite the Village Stores), a few yards east of the Green.

With the windmill on the left go up the field (narrow at first, then opening out behind houses) to cross a piece of fence in the hedge ahead. Go diagonally left across the following field aiming at 11 o'clock and through a gate in the top left-hand hedge near the highest point in the field. Now turn right and diverge gently from the hedge to go through the gate in the hedge ahead. (The waymark on the gate indicates that you have joined the North Bucks Way, a waymarked footpath running from the Chilterns to Milton Keynes.)

Go straight ahead from the gate, climbing the hill but initially keeping below and to the right of the summit; maintain this course for ⅓ mile, walking parallel with the hedge which should be képt 50 yards away on your right.

With every uphill step the view improves. On your right it extends to the dark wall of the Chiltern escarpment while on your left, beyond the faraway cluster of chimneys of the London Brick Company's Calvert brickworks, the land gently rises in the lower slopes of the Cotswolds. As you gain height the surface of the hill becomes pitted by the grass-grown workings and spoil heaps of long-abandoned stone quarries, and the right of way becomes an unworked baulk between pits and spoil heaps.

At the upper end of this field a hedgerow rises from the left across your course. Converge on the right-hand hedge to cross the one in front of you by a broad section of fencing located in the field corner. Bear slightly right in the next field aiming between 12 and 1 o'clock (between the grassy relics of more quarrying) until a pedestrian gate is reached in the hedge on the right (located in a dip, 260 yards beyond the last stile). Pass through the gate and start climbing again, keeping close to the fence on the right until reaching the summit of the ridge ahead (Quainton Hill). Then turn left along the top of the ridge to go through a 5-bar gate in the fence/hedge on the skyline.

Once through the gate you leave the North Bucks Way and continue ahead along the summit of the ridge, following the patchy line of trees on your left, with the chequerboard landscape of North Buckinghamshire spread out below. Ninety yards beyond the last of the line of trees, go through the gate in the fence which appears ahead and continue along the middle of the ridge as it starts to descend.

The roof and chimneys of Upper Hogshaw Farm are seen intermittently below you on the left-hand flank of the ridge. On drawing level with (but still above) the farm buildings, bear left and drop down to go through a gate 80 yards beyond them and on to the farm access track. Follow the track downhill until it meets a road. Turn left along the latter and follow it for ⅓ mile until it ends at a road junction.

> **Just beyond Hill End Farm (on right) the road curves and rises on to an embankment to cross the former route of one of the Metropolitan Railway's remotest branch lines (from Quainton to Verney Junction, the latter just over 50 miles from Baker Street). The branch was built in 1868, taken over by the Metropolitan in 1890, closed to passengers in 1936, and to freight in 1947. The bridge was demolished and the railway cutting to the left of the road filled in during the 1970's, but the course of the line is still visible on the right between two parallel rows of hawthorns.**

At the junction turn left and follow the road for almost ¼ mile. Leave the road by turning left at an "S" bend to go through a wide gateway and continue along a broad, fenced track leading to a group of prefabricated barns.

About 100 yards before reaching the barns, leave the track and climb the fence as you bear half-right to walk to the right-hand corner of the copse ahead (there is a pond beside the corner). Go over the footbridge to pass between pond and copse, then leave an artificial pond to left and continue diagonally across the field (heading just to right of the wireless mast on Quainton Hill) to go through a gate in the middle of the hedge ahead. Continue the same course diagonally to right across the next field, aiming at 1 o'clock and going gently uphill to a gate near the right-hand end of the hedge ahead (Upper Hogshaw Farm is now to your left on the hillside). After going through the gate turn right and aim for the lowest point in the dip between the two hills silhouetted ahead. Leave this field through the small gate in the hedge ahead, seen almost below the dip between the hills just mentioned.

Follow the right-hand hedge along the side of the ensuing field to reach and cross a double stile with a footbridge in the corner of the field; on again in the next, keeping beside the right-hand hedge on slightly rising ground to cross another double stile and footbridge in the next corner. (A group of barns is now on your left below the hill.) Continue in the same general direction, but gradually bear left towards the left-hand hedge to join the track which comes from the barns and follow it through the gate in the corner ahead. Immediately beyond this gate leave the track by going through the gate on the left to cross the field diagonally to a footbridge and stile set in the hedge ahead about 100 yards above the track which you have just left; (ignore the gate about 30 yards further uphill). Go over the stile to walk along a footpath running between hedges. At a "T" junction of paths on the edge of the village turn left, to continue along a fenced path between and through gardens. Finally, on reaching the road, turn left to return to the Green.

Rothschild Country

WADDESDON — WESTCOTT — WADDESDON

Starting point: War Memorial at West (Bicester) end of Waddesdon High Street (A41) immediately west of Five Arrows Hotel (Grid ref: 740168)

Baron Ferdinand de Rothschild bought the Waddesdon Estate from the Duke of Marlborough in 1874. He immediately levelled off the top of Lodge Hill (half a mile south-west of Waddesdon village), and on the flattened hilltop built the magnificent Waddesdon Manor in the style of a Loire Valley chateau. The house was completed in 1881, the bare slopes of the hill were clothed with a vast number of transplanted mature trees, and a landscaped park was laid out around the hill. Rothschild then set about improving the buildings on his estate. In Waddesdon village the seventeenth-century almshouses were modernised, a village hall was built, and the ornate Five Arrows Hotel was erected at one of the entrances to Waddesdon Park. The hotel is named after the Rothschild crest (depicting five crossed arrows), which commemorates the five sons of Mayer Amschel Rothschild (1744–1812) who spread the influence of the original Rothschild banking house of Frankfurt throughout Europe. Buildings throughout the Estate which have been erected or modernised during the Rothschild era carry this crest, and several are seen on this walk.

Waddesdon Manor is open daily (except Mondays and Tuesdays) from the end of March to the end of October; opening times are from 14.00 hours to 18.00 hours. The property is owned by the National Trust.

Travel

Motorists should park in Waddesdon on the broad parking area which flanks the main A41 road at the western end of the village, near the Five Arrows Hotel.

For bus travellers Red Rover's services from Aylesbury to Westcott, Edgcott,

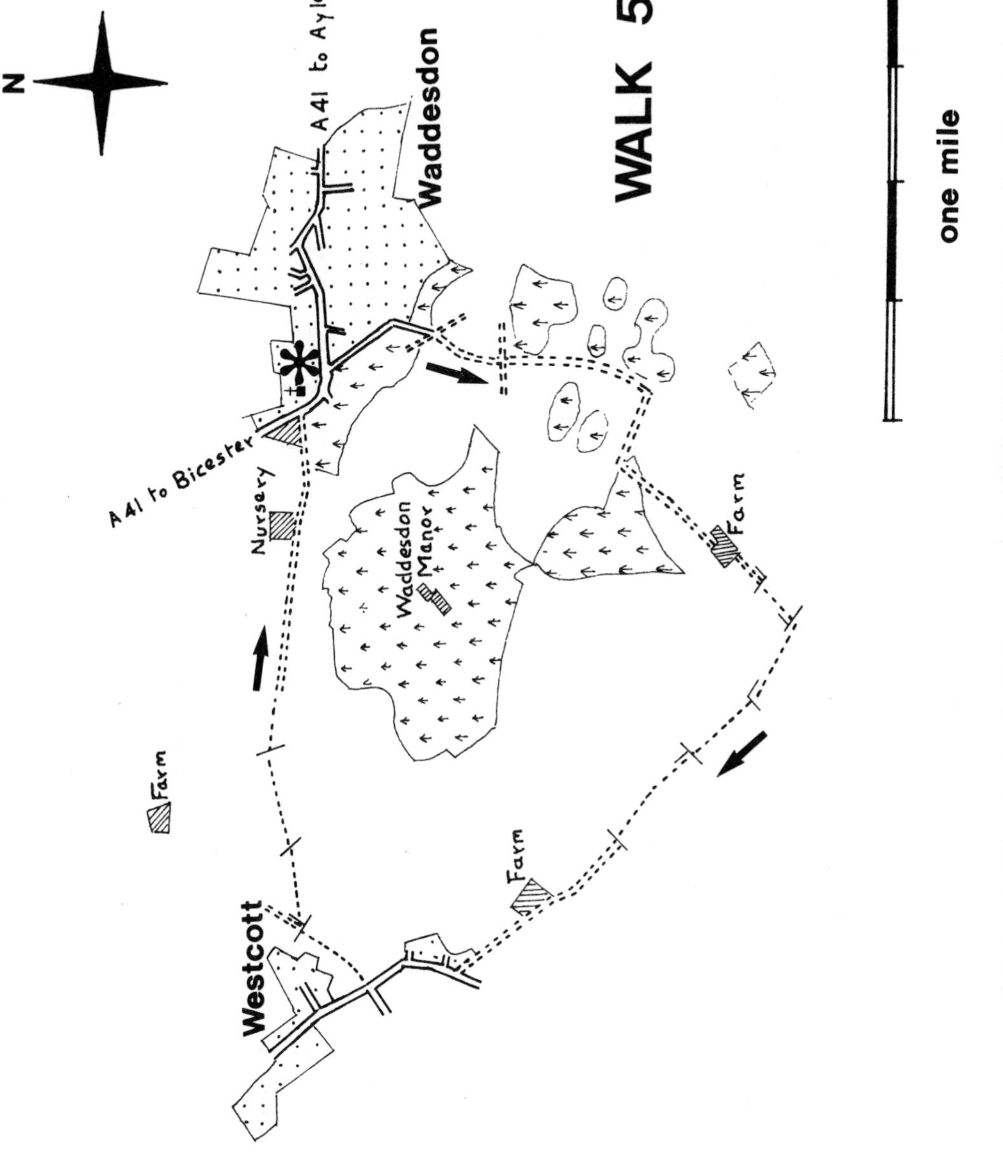

N

A 41 to Aylesbury

Waddesdon

A 41 to Bicester

Nursery

Waddesdon Manor

Farm

Farm

Farm

Westcott

WALK 5

one mile

23

Calvert, and Bicester combine on weekdays to provide a roughly hourly service between Aylesbury and Waddesdon; there is no service on Sundays.

Refreshments

In Waddesdon village there are three pubs and a general store; Westcott has a pub.

Route

Set off from the war memorial along the estate road (which is also a public bridleway) which heads south-eastwards away from the main A41 road. The estate road soon passes between tall brick gate-posts to enter the park of Waddesdon Manor (note the five-arrowed Rothschild crests on the house and estate office just outside the park).

Ignore two crossing estate roads as your route proceeds through the park. Between them the road bears right to pass alongside the village's bowling green and shortly afterwards, as it begins to climb more noticeably, there are brief glimpses of Waddesdon Manor on the tree-clad hill to your right.

Notice here how parts of the parkland have been ploughed up, but that they retain their clumps of trees, planted in the nineteenth century to provide a landscaped setting for the Manor.

Nearly half a mile beyond the bowling green follow the road as it curves sharply to the right and continues to climb (more glimpses of Waddesdon Manor). In another 250 yards it curves sharply left, and (now surfaced in concrete) begins to descend to Windmillhill Farm. On approaching the farm you are now out of the park and in the extensive agricultural lands of the Waddesdon Estate. Follow the metalled route through the farmyard, leaving the farmhouse on your left and turning left, then right, then left and right again, between barns to leave through a gate which gives access to a concrete farm track sloping downhill.

Go down the track, past a pair of semi-detached cottages on the left; then pass through the gate ahead and on downhill in a field beside the fence on your right to go through another gate ahead in the bottom corner of the field.

Once through the latter gate turn right and walk along the upper edge of the field, beside the hedge on your right. Go through the gate in the corner ahead and straight across the following field to leave it through the gate directly in front of you.

Lodge Hill on your right, wooded and crowned by the pinnacles of Waddesdon Manor, was largely treeless just over a century ago. Many of the trees you see today were dug up in nearby parishes and brought here on lumbering horse-drawn

wagons in the 1880's to create an "instantly mature" land-scape around the gleaming new mansion.

On again through two more fields, walking beside the right-hand hedge in the first, and on a track between fence and hedge in the second. After passing through another farm and beside a row of houses this route converges on the road leading through the village of Westcott.

The sports field on your left, just before you converge with the road, was occupied by the gasworks which supplied the Manor from 1883 until 1916. It received coal via a siding off the Brill Tramway (of which, more shortly). A photograph has been published showing railway wagons, the circular gas holder, and the retort house in this field, but all have vanished without trace.

Turn right to follow the road for about ¼ mile. Immediately after the left turn into the Royal Ordnance Factory turn right over the stile beyond the semi-detached pair of cottages ("Station House" and "Station Cottage").

The "station" referred to was Westcott Station on the Brill Tramway, a picturesque but not very successful rural railway which opened in 1871. It ran through thinly-populated country from the main line at Quainton to a terminus at the foot of Brill Hill. Its original purpose was the conveyance of agricultural produce from (and coal to) the Duke of Buckingham's Estate around Wotton House. However the line was acquired by the Metropolitan Railway in 1899, and this, in turn, became part of London Transport when that was formed in 1933. Understandably the Brill Branch did not figure high in the new owner's plans, and it was closed in 1935.

The pair of semi-detached cottages here were built for workers on the Duke's Estate and Tramway (note the "B&C 1871" plaque recalling the Dukes of Buckingham and Chandos); the station building (now somewhat altered) was the lock-up garage on the left side of the cottages.

With the road squarely behind you aim at between 11 and 12 o'clock across the field, following the first overhead electricity line that you meet to the point where it crosses the hedge ahead. Go through the gateway in the hedge into a very short hedged green lane (a section of the route of the old tramway). As soon as you have entered this section, leave it by climbing the stile on your right. The field you are now in is crossed diagonally to left (aiming at 11 o'clock) to go over the stile in the left-hand hedge beneath the *second* of the two overhead electricity lines which cross this field.

Maintain roughly the same course across the following field (with your back to the stile, aim at 1 o'clock) to a gateway which is visible on the skyline when the crop is low. Once through the gateway bear slightly right to continue beside the right-hand fence. This brings you on to the fenced farm track ahead, which is followed back into the village of Waddesdon. (En route you pass the former kitchen gardens and stables of Waddesdon Manor; these are now operated as a nursery garden.)

On reaching the A41 opposite The Bell public house, turn right to return to the starting point.

Millways

Walk 6	4 miles
O.S. 1:25,000 scale map SP70	
(Pathfinder Series 1117)	

HADDENHAM — TYTHROP — SCOTSGROVE MILL — HADDENHAM

Starting point: Church End Green, Haddenham (Grid ref: 741080)

As country footpaths go, this circuit of them is quite busy. The route described is a well-known walk for Haddenham residents and, at its southern end, it shares a path with an equally popular stroll for the people of nearby Thame. In addition the first half mile out of Haddenham is also part of the direct pedestrian link between the villages of Haddenham and Kingsey. It remains a useful short cut between the two because the journey is twice as far by road. All in all we would be surprised if you don't meet anyone while on this walk.

Travel

For bus travellers Oxford Bus and Aylesbury Bus services 2, 260, 280 (Ox- ford–Thame–Aylesbury) combine to give a half-hourly service between Ayles- bury and Thame on weekdays and a 2-hourly service on Sunday afternoons (no service Sunday mornings). Alight at Church End, Haddenham.

For rail travellers there is a daily service at roughly 2-hourly intervals to Haddenham and Thame Parkway station on the Marylebone–High Wycombe– Banbury line. To start the walk turn left out of the station, then first right along Sheerstock and its continuations as Slave Hill and White Cross Road. (Follow the white centre line along these roads to avoid ending in the many culs-de- sac!) At the far end of White Cross Road turn left in Station Road to reach Church End Green.

There is no public car park at Church End, but there is limited room to park considerately on-street in the vicinity.

Refreshments

Only in Haddenham, where you will find pubs and a newsagent/confectioner in Station Road just off Church End Green. In the middle of the village, near to The Crown public house at Fort End, there is a baker's shop and cafe.

Route

Church End Green is surrounded by a pleasant mix of

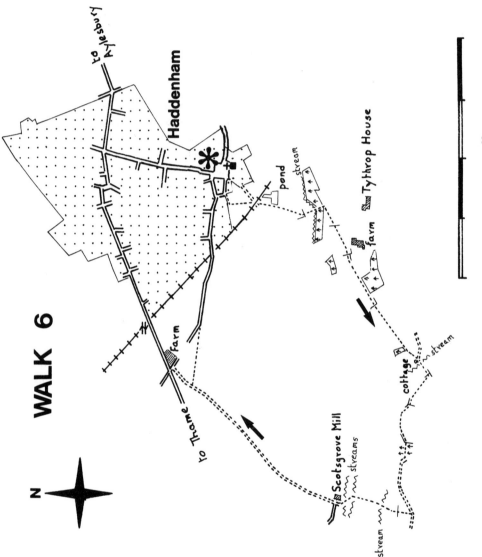

WALK 6

N

Haddenham

to Aylesbury

to Thame

farm

pond

stream

Tythrop House

farm

cottage

stream

Scotsgrove Mill

streams

stream

one mile

buildings from several centuries. Perhaps the oldest is the timber-framed Church Farm House (immediately to left of the church). Its general layout, with a central hall flanked by two-storied wings with projecting upper floors, is a style normally associated with Kent and East Sussex and known as a "Wealden House". Haddenham Manor was held by the Bishops of Rochester from Norman times and this appears to be the reason for this outpost of Kentish architecture.

Start at the war memorial on Church End Green, and set off southwards, leaving the duck pond on your left. Turn first right down Flint Street, and, where it turns sharp right, bear left and take to the footpath which at first runs between traditional witchert walls (see page 50 for details of witchert wall building).

After the path has turned sharp left Manor Farm becomes visible on the left. The farmhouse dates from about 1500 and to the right of it rises the impressively large wooden-walled tithe barn in which the Lord of the Manor stored the Great Tithe (ten per cent of all produce) which he collected from the villagers each year until the practice was ended in 1830.

At the kissing gate at the far end of the hedged section of path go ahead across a small meadow to join the farm track and pass beneath the bridge under the London–High Wycombe–Banbury railway. Just beyond the bridge go through the left-hand of the two gates in front of you to enter a field and continue ahead in it, keeping to the hedge on your right and leaving a pond on your left.

This pond is not a natural one, as is shown by the low embankment which bounds the southern side of it and holds the water in. It is believed that the pond originated in excavations by monks of Rochester Monastery to quarry stone with which to build the church. Having finished their excavations the monks presumably embanked the site to make a fishpond from which to obtain a regular food supply. The modern villagers who pass their days here with rod and line are thus following a long tradition!

Beyond the pond the hedge curves away to the right. Leave it now and bear very slightly left across the field to climb the stile beside a gate in the left-hand corner ahead. This brings you on to a causeway which is slightly raised between two drainage channels. Walk along the causeway, cross a bridge over the stream and go through the narrow belt of woodland known as Hook

Covert. The gate on the far side of the Covert brings you into a field which slopes gently uphill in the parish of Kingsey.

The mansion visible ahead is Tythrop House, which dates from the late seventeenth century, and was long the home of the Wykeham family. They sold it in 1933 and, after a period of vacancy, it was occupied by refugees from the Spanish Civil War. With the onset of World War II the refugees were replaced by the Royal Army Service Corps. After the war the house became a private home once again and, over a period of 25 years, was painstakingly restored to the superb condition in which you see it today.

Immediately beyond the gate bear right at 2 o'clock and cross two fields diagonally towards the large modern farm buildings, leaving Tythrop House well on your left. Cross the stile in the middle of the fence between these fields and pass just to the left of a grassy hollow (the site of a long-disused quarry) in the second field.

On reaching the farm buildings stay in the field and carry on past them to the stile between a pair of gates in the fence ahead situated just in front of an overhead electricity line. Climb the stile and continue ahead, passing a pair of cottages and keeping close beside the fence on your left. Soon you are walking alongside a small wood on your left.

At the far end of the field cross the stile in the fence in front of you and maintain the same direction of travel across the middle of the ensuing field, aiming for the right-hand end of the cottage roof which is visible in the trees ahead. (If a standing crop hides the cottage, project forward the line of the fence you have just been walking beside and head for the vee-shaped gap in the trees at which this line points.)

Far away to the left the horizon is formed by the line of the Chiltern Hills, with British Telecom's 320 ft-high Stokenchurch Telecommunications Tower standing prominently on top.

On reaching the first corner of the small copse, pass the kissing gate which marks the site of a former fence line. Continue to the next corner of the wood then bear slightly left downhill across the field to a stile in the fence immediately to left of the cottage. This brings you on to a farm track.

Bear right along the track past the cottage (the initials PJDW 1897 which can be seen on it refer to the Wykeham family, former owners of Tythrop Park). Cross a brick bridge over a tributary of the Scotsgrove Brook, go through the gate, and continue (now in Oxfordshire) along the tree-lined causeway across a meadow which is liable to flooding in winter; it ends at a gate with a stile on the right-hand side of it.

This causeway was in use as part of the private carriageway between Thame and Tythrop House before the modern Thame–Princes Risborough Road (which runs parallel, some 500 yards to the left) was built as a Turnpike in 1825.

Turn right over the stile to set off in a new direction, curving along the right-hand margin of two fields following a drainage ditch on your right. After about 250 yards in the second field go through the small gate which appears in front of you in a corner and follow a path through the thicket ahead. On emerging from the far end of the thicket bear right to follow a grass baulk which becomes a track along the curving right-hand margin of a large, gently-sloping field.

After some 600 yards an overhead electricity line crosses the track in front of you (and beyond it the track becomes fenced on both sides). One hundred yards *before* reaching the electricity line turn right to enter a field through the last gate before the line. Head slightly to the right across the field, to cross a farm access bridge in a gap near the middle of the hedge ahead. Maintain the same course in the following field until you have crossed a stream by means of a concrete bridge (whose handrails are visible above the meadow). Then change direction slightly to left and head across the meadows towards the small group of buildings at Scotsgrove Mill which are visible ahead in the trees. About 80 yards before reaching the Mill, cross a stream (which forms the county boundary) by means of another concrete bridge. Then follow the hedge on left and cross the roaring millrace on a brick bridge at the corner of the Mill buildings.

There has been a water mill at Scotsgrove for at least 900 years. The Domesday Survey records the presence of two water mills in Haddenham in 1066 but in the opinion of Walter Rose, Haddenham's local historian, this is due to there being two water wheels in the same building at Scotsgrove.

The several successive water mills on this site ground Haddenham's corn throughout this long period, although as the village's population grew, they came to be supplemented by windmills in other parts of the parish. Scotsgrove Mill was last used commercially in 1967, having been run by the Freeman family since the mid-nineteenth century, and after this date the building stood empty until being converted into a dwelling in the early 1970's. The Mill came into prominence again in 1972 when an attempt to divert the public path away from it was successfully opposed by the people of Haddenham.

Once over the mill stream continue along the track beside the Mill buildings. Ignore the narrow road going off on the left, and carry on straight ahead up the bridleway.

This bridleway which, appropriately, is listed as "Haddenham No. 1" on the modern Definitive Map of public footpaths, is perhaps the most important of the historic fieldpaths of Haddenham Parish. It was in existence long before the construction of the modern Haddenham–Thame road which now parallels it, and was followed by countless generations of Haddenham folk as they went to and from the Mill — they called it "Millways".

The bridleway gradually converges on the Haddenham–Thame road, and joins it at the crossroads beside the large modern farm barns which become visible ahead. For this walk, however, turn right over the stile which is found in the fence 200 yards short of the barns, where the bridleway bends slightly to left, just beyond the bottom of a shallow dip. Having climbed the stile head slightly to left at between 11 and 12 o'clock across the field, aiming just to the left of the short row of trees which can be seen in front of the left-hand end of the visible part of the Chiltern escarpment. (As you come over the gentle rise in this field you will see and aim for the gates leading on to Station Road, ahead on left.)

Leave the field over the stile beside the double gates and turn right along Station Road to return to Haddenham.

Station Road was formerly known as White Cross Road and it only acquired its present name after the opening of the railway through Haddenham in 1906. The name of White Cross Road was revived in 1975 for a new residential road which you pass on your left just beyond the railway.

It was in 1963 that most of the local stations on the railway between Princes Risborough and Banbury were closed. Two years before closure Haddenham station saw a daily average of 31 passengers joining trains from its platforms, which compared favourably with Ilmer's 2 passengers but was insufficient to retain the rail service. The station stood in the cutting on the left of the railway bridge until it was demolished in 1978 and its site used to create a recreation ground.

As Haddenham's population grew in the 1970's and 1980's it became apparent that the village and surrounding area might be able to support a station again. One was opened in 1987 on a new site, several hundred yards to north of the old site, as a

**result of which the station is now in Thame Road, and Station
Road has no station!**

Follow the road over the railway bridge and back into the village until it ends at Church End Green.

Castle Patrol

WHITCHURCH — HARDWICK — ASTON ABBOTTS PARISH BOUNDARY — WHITCHURCH

Starting point: North end of Whitchurch High Street, at junction with Market Hill (Grid ref: 801209)

Whitchurch was once a market town in the shadow of a castle; it was granted a market charter in 1245. Today Market Hill widens into a grassy space where traders once assembled and although earthworks mark the site of the castle, there are no walls remaining. Long ago the market was overtaken by the one at Aylesbury but Whitchurch, with its narrow streets sloping off the High Street, retains the feel of a country town while remaining small enough to be a village. It has more than its share of historic buildings and these ensure that it has a distinct character that makes one want to wander round it in spite of the through traffic which roars along the High Street.

Travel

Red Rover service 2 (Aylesbury–Buckingham) and Aylesbury Bus service 66 (Aylesbury–Buckingham–Akeley) combine to give roughly *an hourly service to Whitchurch on weekdays. There is no Sunday service.*

Cars can be parked in the lay-bys on both sides of the south (Aylesbury) end of the High Street.

Refreshments

Whitchurch has pubs, a baker and a grocer in High Street. Hardwick has a pub.

Route

Start near the north end of the village, where Market Hill leaves High Street (A413). Follow Market Hill and, when it forks, bear left along Castle Lane. 80 yards beyond the fork leave the road just beyond the thatched cottage by going over the stile on left (located between two gates). Now set off with the road squarely behind you, following for a short distance the grassy platform with a sharp drop on left and a grassy mound on right.

WALK 7

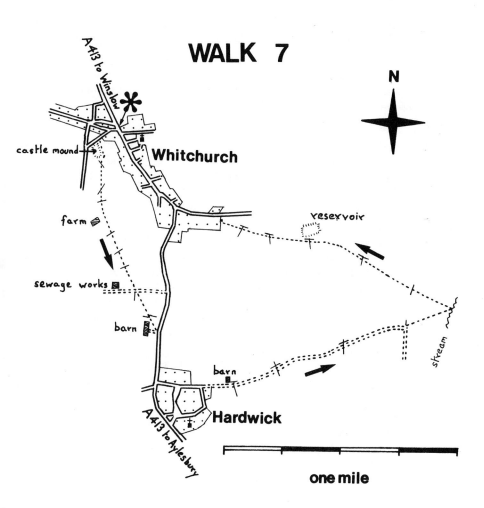

The grassy mound is the motte, or elevated inner area, of the former Bolebec Castle; the rampart you are on marks the line of its outer defences. When built (probably in the eleventh century) the castle had a stone-built tower and perimeter wall on the mound and a moat round its base (now silted up, on your right). It was already ruinous by the time of the Civil War when it was held for the Royalists, as a result of which it was laid waste by the Roundheads. In the following years it became a quarry of building material for local people, and stones from the castle have been used in repairs to a number of the older Whitchurch houses.

90 yards after leaving the road, a feintly visible footpath starts to drop obliquely down the side of the rampart (just before you pass a telegraph pole in the field below on left). Follow this path down to "ground level", crossing a brook issuing from a spring in the ramparts. Then curve to right around a sector of the base of the rampart to go through the gate in the field boundary which soon appears ahead. Now turn left, at between 9 and 10 o'clock from the gate, to walk downhill for 180 yards, with the tree-clad mass of the castle behind you. Watch carefully for a footbridge flanked by stiles in the left-hand hedge (it is near the lowest part of the field, just beyond the lone telegraph pole visible close behind the hedge). Cross the bridge and aim at 2 o'clock across the next field to go through the gateway in the hedge ahead (seen 30 yards to left of the next telegraph pole).

Straight ahead across the lower end of the next field, to cross the stiles and footbridge which become visible in the hedge opposite. Maintain the same course across the following two fields, using a gate between them and stiles and a footbridge on the far side of the second. Aim diagonally at 11 o'clock across the ensuing field, leaving a small sewage works well to right, and go out through the gate in the far left corner. Once through the gate turn sharp right and immediately go through the double gates beside you.*

Cross the concrete access track, go through the gates opposite and traverse the following field diagonally to left aiming straight for the tower of Hardwick Church (seen to left of the large farm barn in foreground). Climb the fence ahead and maintain the same course across a final field to come out on to the main road via a stile in the left-hand hedge, found beside the gate in the field corner. Cross the A413 and turn right to follow its pavement for 350 yards to reach the turning to Hardwick.

For notes on Hardwick, please see page 123

---

*These gates are slightly to left of the legal line of path. Hopefully, during the currency of this book, stiles will be provided to take you across the track ahead.

Turn left up the road into the village and follow it over the green and on downhill. Where the metalled road turns right, beside a remarkably small war memorial, keep straight on, now on a clearly-defined farm track which winds along the left-hand side of three fields, crossing cattle grids between them, and then along the right-hand side of a fourth.

As you follow this wide, shallow valley, three villages are partially visible on the skyline — Whitchurch to left, Aston Abbotts straight ahead, and Weedon to right.

At the end of the fourth field the track turns away to right. Leave it and aim at 11 o'clock across the following field (heading just to left of the sky-line barns). This course brings you to a long footbridge leading into Aston Abbotts parish beyond the stream. However this walk does not go over the water. Once at the bridge turn around and, with your back to it, recross the field, now heading for the piece of fencing in a gap in the opposite hedge. This fencing is immediately to left of the telegraph pole in the *next* field, located just behind the hedge; there is a wide sleeper bridge in front of the fencing.

Cross the fencing and maintain almost the same course uphill across the next field, passing obliquely beneath the overhead electricity line and converging on the right-hand hedge to join it in the top right-hand corner (at the uphill end of a row of hedgerow trees). Cross the stile in the corner and continue ahead, uphill at first, along the right-hand edge of four fields.

As you reach the summit in the second of these four fields a wide panorama opens up with the Chiltern Hills forming the far skyline to the south while, nearer at hand, the wooded hill on which Waddesdon Manor stands is ahead at 11 o'clock. Brill Hill is beyond it. On your right can be seen the forest of telegraph masts at the Diplomatic Wireless Relay Station at Creslow. The large and suspiciously rectangular grass mound in the field on right at the summit is unsuccessfully trying to hide a water storage tank.

In the fourth field continue beside the right-hand hedge to reach the first house in Whitchurch. Go through the gate in the corner beside the house and down a short track to reach the road. Turn left along the road, then right when it meets Whitchurch's High Street. After passing the White Swan public house and the "S" bend you come into the historic part of the High Street, with its rich variety of buildings from various centuries. You have almost arrived back at your starting point, but for a further view of Whitchurch turn up White Horse Lane (third turning on right after the White Swan) and into the churchyard.

On your right in the churchyard, opposite the chancel, is the

small stone tablet recording the villagers' relief in 1972, when the Government decided against building the Third London Airport at Cublington, a few miles to the east of Whitchurch.

The church itself dates partly from the thirteenth and fourteenth centuries. It is faced with heavily weathered stone and has a sense of peace which would have gone by now if the airport had been built.

Turn left in front of the south porch, then immediately right past the church tower and out of the churchyard to turn left along Church Headland Lane to return to the High Street.

In Cromwell's Footsteps

STEEPLE CLAYDON — HILLESDEN — KING'S BRIDGE — STEEPLE CLAYDON

Starting point: Steeple Claydon Parish Church (Grid ref: 705267)

The English Civil War (1642–46) lacked the clearly-defined front lines of classic international conflicts. Although the armies of Parliament and the King met in full battle in several locations, much of the war consisted of skirmishes between soldiers sallying forth from the strategic towns garrisoned by one side or the other. One such attack took place at the isolated village of Hillesden, where the principal buildings were the church and the adjoining Hillesden House. Hillesden, the seat of the Denton family, stood in the no-man's-land between Charles I's temporary capital at Oxford, and the Parliamentary garrisons at Aylesbury and Newport Pagnell.

In February 1644 Sir Alexander Denton, a Royalist, began to fortify Hillesden by digging a ditch-and-bank earthwork encircling the church and his house. Hearing of this, the Parliamentarians sent a small force from Aylesbury on 28 February to take Hillesden and thereby prevent the completion of the defences. The attack was beaten off, but several days later a force of 2,000 men, half of them commanded by Colonel Oliver Cromwell, marched to Steeple Claydon, spent the night there, and then attacked Hillesden House on the morning of 4 March 1644.

Although the precise route of Cromwell's army from Steeple Claydon to Hillesden is not recorded, the two legs of this walk follow the two most likely routes to have been used.

Travel

Red Rover services 15 (Aylesbury–Calvert) and 16 (Aylesbury–Bicester) serve Steeple Claydon with infrequent buses on weekdays (best on Wednesdays and Saturdays). There is no Sunday service. It is perfectly possible to travel to

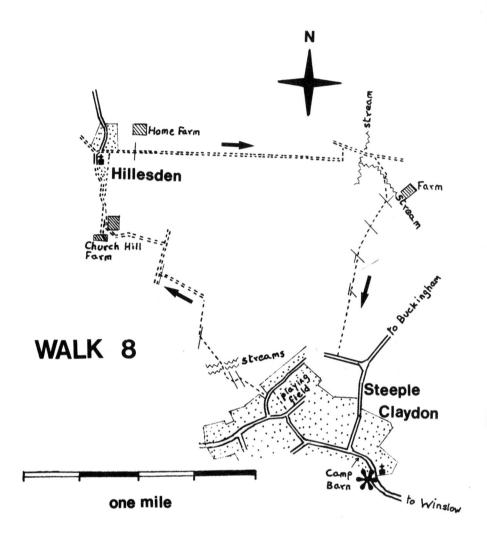

N

Home Farm

Hillesden

stream

Farm

stream

Church Hill
Farm

to Buckingham

WALK 8

streams

Steeple
Claydon

playing
field

one mile

Camp
Barn

to Winslow

and from the walk on these services, but check times with Red Rover before setting out. Alight at Steeple Claydon church.

Motorists can park on the broad area of road in front of the parish church.

Refreshments

These are only found in Steeple Claydon, where there are pubs and grocery shops.

Route

Start on the edge of Steeple Claydon at the parish church and set off along the road into the village.

> Two hundred yards from the church look out for the pair of
> barns on left. The old, stone one which projects towards the
> road is Camp Barn. Around this building, on the night of 3/4
> March 1644, 2,000 men of the Parliamentary army camped
> before their dawn departure for Hillesden under the com-
> mand of Sir Samuel Luke and Colonel Oliver Cromwell. The
> garden containing the barn still bears traces of the defensive
> earthworks around the camp; some can be seen from the gate
> as you pass.

Ignore the right turn to Buckingham and continue ahead along Queen
Catherine Road and on down Chaloners Hill. At the bottom of the hill, when
the main village road swings sharp left and becomes West Street, turn right
into Meadoway and immediately left down the metalled footpath which starts
between The Old School House and the playing field and continues beside
new houses. When it ends at the next road, turn left along it for 40 yards, then
turn right to follow a fenced footpath out of the village.

The path ends at a stile leading into the next field. Go straight across this
field, climb the stile in the hedge ahead then bear sharp right to pass to the
left of the small brick-built pumping station and go down to the right-hand
corner of the field. Ahead now across the two footbridges spanning channels
of the Claydon Brook. Cross the first field beyond the stream diagonally at 11
o'clock to a stile midway along the left-hand hedge (an overhead electricity
line post stands immediately behind the stile). Cross the stile and turn right to
walk along the right-hand margin of the next field.

> Behind the clump of trees on the summit of the low hill on left
> is Hillesden church, objective of Cromwell's troops on that
> March morning.

In the field corner ahead stay in this field and turn left onto a farm track
which runs along the next side of the field heading straight for the farm
buildings on the hill. The track emerges into the bottom side of a large field
sloping up to the farm. Turn right with the track along the bottom of this field
to reach its corner, then left in the same field to follow the track uphill to the
farm barns.

Stay on the track as it curves to run between the farm barns and farm
house, and then on towards Hillesden church. When the fence on right gives
way to a hedge (half way between farm and church) climb the stile into the
field on right. Once over the stile bear left to walk up the field following the
hedge on left. When you reach the two modern houses on left continue in the
same direction (now beside a garden wall) to climb the stile in the fence ahead
(immediately to right of the church wall) and come on to an access road.

> Pause as you pass the church. The hummocky field in which

you are standing is the site of Hillesden House (note the bricked-up access gateway in the churchyard wall and the filled-in end of a bridge from the church at first-floor level). The new earthworks which ringed church and house on 4 March 1644 were incomplete when the Parliamentary force arrived at 9 a.m. The 263 defenders were no match for 2,000 attackers and quickly fell back into the house and church. After further fighting the Royalists surrendered. On the following day rumours of the approach of a Royalist counter attack from Oxford led Cromwell to order the burning of Hillesden House. It was left in ruins.

To continue your walk climb the stile ahead and turn right along the access road. First, however, you may wish to turn left through the gateway to visit the church.

Hillesden church is a masterpiece of the late Perpendicular period, having been built in its present form in about 1500. The church door is pitted with what are claimed as bullet holes from the 1644 attack. In the churchyard a tall, heavily weathered, octagonal stone column marks the mass grave of 30 Royalists who were wantonly murdered by the victors immediately after the surrender on 4 March.

Return through the gateway and set off along the access road with the buildings of Home Farm on left and the gardens of the modern (1970's) Hillesden House on right. As you come over the brow of the hilltop, a long straight avenue appears ahead, dropping down into the valley of the Claydon Brook. Climb the stile beside the gate in front of you and walk the full mile-long length of the avenue.

As soon as the Civil War was over the Denton family demolished the ruins of the first Hillesden House and built a second one on its site. In due course the new house was set in landscaped gardens and provided with this grand avenue. It replaced the earlier track which ran from Hillesden down to the Buckingham–London road, which it joined on the far side of the Claydon Brook, less than two miles away. During the turnpike era that main road was superseded by the route which became the modern A413, running further to the east, and the second Hillesden House was demolished without replacement. The avenue thus became redundant but it is pleasing to see that the present owners are replanting the rows of trees which once made it such a distinctive feature.

At the foot of the avenue follow it as it swings sharp left and ends in front of a gate. Climb the stile beside the gate and turn right along the path running between hedges down to the King's Bridge over the Claydon Brook. Cross the bridge and continue along the hedged path (the former road) beyond for 100 yards; take care to go no further!*

Look carefully to find the not-very-obvious piece of fencing acting as a stile in a gap in the right-hand hedge, 100 yards beyond the bridge. Cross the fencing and bear diagonally left across the field, heading for the right-hand side of the barns of Kingsbridge Farm. This course brings you to walk beside the opposite hedge (after it has turned a corner), and the deep stream flowing beside it. Cross the stream on the footbridge 100 yards before the farm. Once over it bear left at between 10 and 11 o'clock across the ensuing field to the gate in the far corner (close to an electricity line pole in the hedge). Go straight across the following field (with the overhead electricity line diverging to left) and through the large gap in the hedge ahead.

Pause at the gap, standing on the upper side of a sloping field, with Steeple Claydon on the skyline ahead to the left. Look at the hedge across the bottom of the field you are now in and locate the hedge climbing away from behind it towards the middle of Steeple Claydon. Now set off to cross the field you are in, aiming slightly left downhill to reach the junction of the two hedges just mentioned.

Cross the stile and footbridge at the hedge junction at the bottom of the field and continue uphill, along the right-hand side of two fields, keeping beside the hedge referred to in the previous paragraph. A stile in the far right-hand corner of the second of these fields brings you out on to a road. Turn left along the road to the "T" junction, then right to follow the Buckingham Road uphill into Steeple Claydon.

When Buckingham Road ends at a "T" junction, turn left to return to the church.

---

*If this path is very muddy, use the "tunnel" cut by the Winslow Ramblers in the thick left-hand hedge; it starts 30 yards beyond the bridge, runs just above the mud level, and ends in 70 yards.

The Preachers' Path?

Walk 9	5 miles
O.S. 1:25,000 scale maps SP81, 82	
(Pathfinder Series 1071, 1094)	

WING — ASTON ABBOTTS — ROWSHAM

Starting point: Wing Parish Church (Grid ref: 880225)

For much of its length this route follows the crest of a low, rounded jumble of hills which run from east to west across this part of the Vale of Aylesbury. Consequently, although you are never more than 200 ft above the base level of the Vale, this walk enjoys an unusual variety of scenery. In fact the only consistent feature of the walk is the dark wall of the Chilterns which is visible away to the south for most of your journey.

Travel

For motorists there is a small (say 6 cars) parking area in a widening of Church Street beside the church in Wing. If you park here you can catch a bus back from the end of the walk.

Travel by bus to Wing and alight at The Dove public house. Follow High Street past the Post Office and turn left into Church Street to reach the parish church and the start of this walk. Bus services on weekdays are at intervals varying between 1 and 2 hours on Aylesbury Bus/Bee Line joint services X14, X15 (Reading–High Wycombe–Aylesbury–Leighton Buzzard–Milton Keynes) and Aylesbury Bus route 65 (Aylesbury–Leighton Buzzard). On Sundays the 65 and X14 do not run and the X15 only runs one bus in the afternoon and one in the evening.

Refreshments

Wing has two grocery shops, a confectioner, a Tea Room and three pubs in the High Street. Aston Abbotts has a pub and a grocery shop almost facing each other. There are no facilities at Rowsham.

Route

Wing parish church is of national importance as a rare survival of Saxon architecture. The original church on the site (parts of which still stand today) may have been put up as early as the seventh century. It was built as a minster church

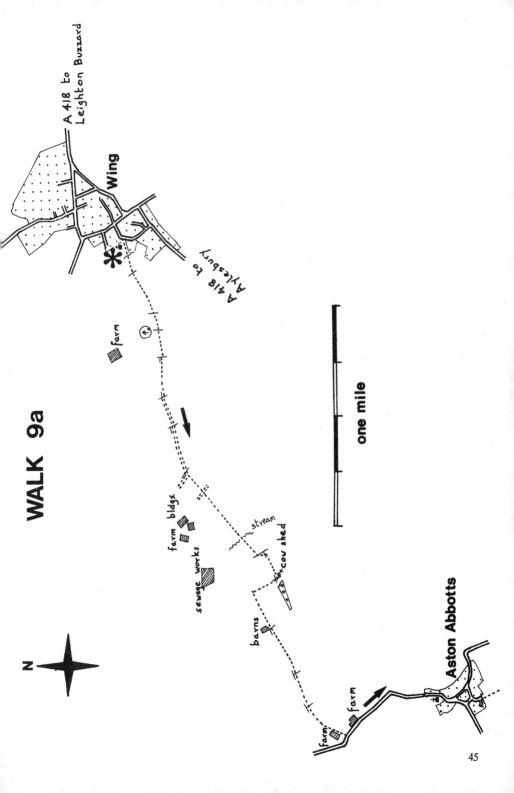

WALK 9a

N

A 418 to Leighton Buzzard

Wing

A 418 to Aylesbury

farm

farm bldgs

sewage works

stream

cow shed

barns

farm

farm

Aston Abbotts

one mile

45

at a time before the modern network of parish churches was established in England. Minster churches housed monks who went out to preach in the open air in the surrounding churchless communities from roughly the seventh to the tenth centuries. Gradually other churches came to be built as villages grew large enough to need them and their lords of the manor became wealthy enough to afford them. As this happened, the travelling monks from the minsters were replaced by resident priests in the village churches and the role of the minster churches ended by the early twelfth century.

Set off along the metalled footpath which runs through the churchyard, with the church on your *right*. Go through the gate at the end of the churchyard and straight ahead, downhill across the first field, to go over the double stile in the middle of the hedge ahead. In the following field move a few paces to right, then resume your course, following a shallow hollow way up the low hill ahead and down to cross the footbridge in the hedge on its far side. (As you descend the hill a large group of farm buildings should be to your right, nearly half a mile away.)

The complex but generally symmetrical earthworks on right at the bottom of the field are a puzzle. They are too far above the adjoining stream to have been water-filled, and are too regular to be the results of quarrying.

Continue across the next field to go over the stile/footbridge immediately to right of the gate in the hedge ahead. On again, up the middle of the next field, to go through the gate on the skyline ahead, and maintain the same course, now beside a fence on your right, along the side of the following field. Cross the stile in the corner ahead and continue the same course across the middle of the ensuing field, walking on a grassy farm track. Follow the track through the gap in the hedge ahead and on along the right-hand side of the next field, beside the hedge. At the next corner the track turns right. Leave it here, and change direction very slightly left uphill across the ensuing field, aiming at about 2 minutes to 12 o'clock to reach a farm track crossing your route on the far side of the field; on this course you very slowly diverge from the left-hand hedge so that it is 60 yards away when you enter the field and 100 yards away when you reach the crossing track.

The rather run-down collection of prefabricated buildings to right are now used for agriculture but started life as living accommodation and stores for RAF Wing, a wartime Bomber Command aerodrome opened in 1941 on land out of sight to the north.

Cross the farm track leading to the farm buildings on right and maintain your course across the next field, now very slowly converging on the left-hand hedge, which starts off 100 yards away. This course brings you over the summit and down to a broad gateway and tractor bridge in the hedge ahead, about 60 yards from the field's left-hand corner.

As you descend the field the squat brick building of the local sewage works (ahead on right) strikes an intrusive note in the countryside.

Go over the bridge and straight ahead uphill across the next field to cross the stile and footbridge directly in front of you in the hedge on the skyline. Now turn sharp left to reach the next corner of the field, and there cross the footbridge and stile in front of you. Once over the stile turn right to walk along the right-hand side of the field towards a small brick and timber cow shed.

Go through the gate in the corner to right of the cow shed and promptly turn right to continue along the right-hand side of the following field to its next corner. There turn left to follow its boundary again to reach the corner near to an isolated pair of farm barns. Go through the gate in that corner and ahead beside the hedge along the right-hand side of the ensuing three fields to come out on to the Aston Abbotts–Cublington road through a gate in the corner of the third field (between two farms). Turn left to walk ½ mile along the road into Aston Abbotts.

The present church at Aston Abbotts dates from 1865 but its predecessor was apparently built in the early Norman period. We can speculate that, in the three or four centuries between the coming of Christianity to England and the building of that church, the monks of Wing Minster would have come here, possibly using the route you have just walked, to preach on the village green. (By the way, the "Abbotts" in the village's name relates to the period when the Manor was owned by St. Albans Abbey, and does not commemorate the visits of the Wing monks.)

On reaching the village green, take the road forking right across it (signposted to Weedon); after 100 yards turn left off the Weedon road (the left turn is still called The Green) and in another 70 yards turn right into Bricstock. Enter the playing field ahead through the gate facing you across the end of Bricstock. Go straight across the field to leave it over the fence 5 yards to left of the gate directly in front of you (not immediately visible).

This brings you into the upper corner of a sloping field. Keep to the hedge along the right-hand side of this and the following field. Once over the

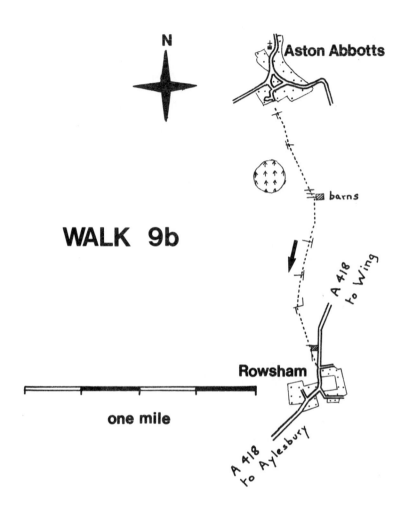

WALK 9b

N

Aston Abbotts

barns

A 418 to Wing

Rowsham

A 418 to Aylesbury

one mile

summit of the second field, diverge slightly from the hedge to go through the gate in the fence across your route.

> **Just before reaching the gate, the very extensive view which opens up on the right extends for more than 20 miles (if visibility is clear) on to the lower slopes of the Cotswolds in the Woodstock area.**

Continue straight ahead across the next field to climb the stile located a little to right of the isolated group of hilltop barns. On again, passing the barns on your left to climb the fence ahead and set off up the left-hand side of the large sloping field beyond.

In the first 50 yards beyond the barns another panorama opens up to right.

In the field corner ahead cross the stile in front of you, then continue along the left-hand side of the following two fields, now with views extending to the detached "knob" of Ivinghoe Beacon in the Chilterns on far left.

With the hamlet of Rowsham now appearing ahead (below to left), go through the gate in the hedge/fence ahead at the far end of the second field (slightly to right of your line of travel) and on down the right-hand side of the third field. Leave it through the left-hand one of two gates facing you, just behind the nearest house in Rowsham. Immediately beyond the house climb the fence on left and cross the paddock diagonally to its far left-hand corner, where you emerge on the A413.

Turn right for a few paces to the bus stop for Aylesbury (on other side of road) or continue a few yards more on this side of the road for the stop for Wing and Leighton Buzzard-bound buses.

If you would like to walk further towards Aylesbury, turn to page 127 for the route description from Rowsham to Hulcott (¾ mile). On reaching Hulcott walk on another ½ mile by minor road, passing the church on your left, to reach Bierton on the outskirts of Aylesbury, where buses X14, X15, and 65 call.

The Witchert Villages

Walk 10	6 miles
O.S. 1:25,000 scale maps SP70, 71	
(Pathfinder Series 1093, 1117)	

HADDENHAM — CHEARSLEY — NOTLEY — HADDENHAM

Starting point: The Crown p.h., Fort End, Haddenham (Grid ref: 740088)

For centuries the villages of Dinton, Westlington, Chearsley,
Cuddington, and Haddenham have used mud walling called
witchert (a mixture of chopped straw with local clay) as a
building material. Today the older parts of these villages
are still characterised by the tile-capped witchert garden
walls, and the irregular appearance of witchert buildings.
This irregularity results from the flexibility of the building material which allows virtually random arrangement of
windows, and tends to make all corners a little rounded and
wall faces a little uneven. Witchert is normally covered with
white-washed rendering for protection against the weather,
but there are plenty of garden walls which have lost their
rendering to expose the stone foundation (the "grumpling")
and the 2 ft-high courses of witchert (called "berries") lying
above it.

This walk passes through two of the witchert villages.

Travel

*Motorists should use the car park behind the Village Hall (entrance from
Banks Road opposite east end of modern shopping parade). (Banks Road, in
the middle of the village, is part of the principal east–west route through
Haddenham.) After parking, walk west along Banks Road for 200 yards to
Fort End for the start of the walk.*

*Bus travellers have Oxford Bus and Aylesbury Bus services 2, 260, and 280
(Oxford–Thame–Aylesbury) which combine to give a half-hourly service
between Thame and Aylesbury on weekdays and a 2-hourly interval on Sunday
afternoons (no service Sunday mornings). Alight from all buses at The Crown,
Fort End, Haddenham.*

*Rail travellers arriving at Haddenham & Thame Parkway Station on the
Marylebone–High Wycombe–Banbury line, must turn left out of the station
and follow the dead straight road into the village for ²/₃ mile to reach The*

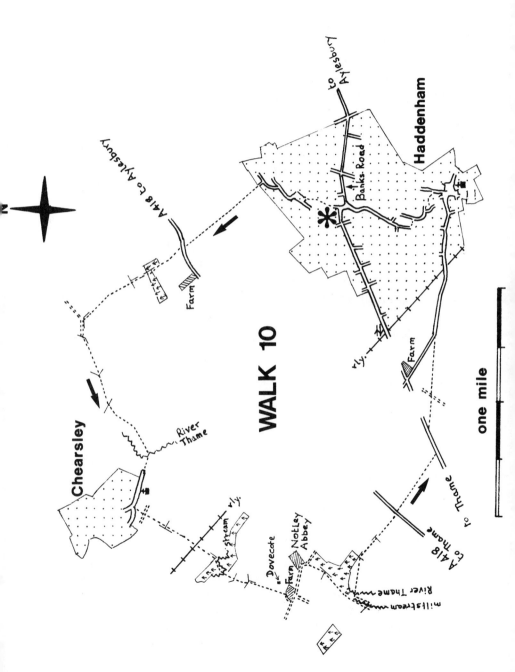

WALK 10

Haddenham

Chearsley

to Aylesbury

A418 to Aylesbury

Banks Road

Farm

Farm

rly.

River Thame

River Thame

Millstream

Dovecote

Farm Notley Abbey

Stream

rly.

A418 to Thame

to Thame

one mile

N

51

Crown public house, at Fort End. The train service is roughly 2-hourly every day.

Refreshments

There is a fish and chip shop (open lunch-times and evenings on Tuesdays to Saturdays) in the Banks Road shopping parade at Haddenham, and a baker's shop and cafe at the start of this walk in Fort End. In addition there are pubs in Haddenham and Chearsley.

Route

The old part of Haddenham, with its three greens and duckponds, stretches sinuously for nearly a mile along the banks of a stream from Church End (in the south), through Fort End, to Towns End. Postwar housing development has greatly enlarged the village on both sides of its mediaeval north–south spine, but you can still capture the old atmosphere of witchert walls and thatched roofs at the end of this ramble as you walk along the narrow lanes and high-walled footpaths whch link the "Ends".

Start at Fort End, Haddenham, a meeting point of some five roads in the middle of the village (with The Crown public house on one corner).

Set off down Fern Lane, the cul-de-sac leading northwards out of Fort End, and, at the head of the Lane, continue in the same direction along the metalled footpath which starts on the left of the "Old Brewery". (Note witchert walls bounding the path in some places, and modern imitations in others.) At the end of the path bear left to go diagonally across Towns End Green and join the road at the far left corner of the green; follow the road round an "S" bend into Rudds Lane, then turn left into Rosemary Lane and, a little further on, left again down a short drive leading to "Cobweb", a thatched cottage with an attractive cluster of circular brick chimneys.

Where the drive swings right into the gates of "Cobweb" go ahead over a stile, and along the narrow grassy baulk, which carries a patchy hedge and which runs straight between fields for nearly half a mile. At the end of the baulk, go through the gap in the hedge ahead, cross the A418, and enter the left-hand of two fields opposite.

Immediately upon entering the field, note the *very* slight mound beside you on your left. This is all that remains of Roundhill, a large artificial mound which, in the eighteenth century, measured 74 yards in circumference at its base and 37 yards in circumference at its summit. The slope of its sides was 4 yards long and on its top was an indentation in the

shape of a cross. It was destroyed in the nineteenth century, but was not excavated prior to destruction so the secret of its purpose has vanished with it. Walter Rose, a local historian, suggested that it was a pagan burial place, and possibly a meeting place at which the villagers of Haddenham, Cuddington, Chearsley and Dinton met officials touring the district in Saxon times. Certainly there is little left today which is suggestive of the importance of this site in the past, but the name is perpetuated at Roundhill Farm, which is visible on the left across the field.

Once over the stile maintain your previous direction, keeping to the fence/ hedge on the right, first on the level, then downhill to the coppice ahead. In the bottom right-hand corner of the field go straight ahead over the stile, down the path through the coppice, and over another stile into the field beyond. Continue ahead beside the ditch along the right-hand side of the field, to reach the gate/stile in the corner ahead. Cross the stile and strike uphill across the next field, aiming at between 12 and 1 o'clock towards the nearest point of a group of low trees which projects out into the field on the skyline.

On reaching the above point (a projecting corner of the boundary fence) nearly at the top of the hill, ignore a stile visible some yards away on your right and bear slightly left to go forward over the summit and downhill, beside the right-hand hedge/fence; the village of Chearsley is now visible on the left on the far side of the valley. When you arrive at the first corner at the bottom of the field cross the stile beside the gate to leave the field. Then turn sharp left and continue on the track running along the bottom of the field for 90 yards to go over the stile beside the gate ahead of you. Now bear slightly left and walk downhill, crossing the rolling ridge-and-furrow obliquely, and making for a pair of gates in the far corner. Pass through the right-hand gate and continue in the same direction across the next field, crossing it diagonally and heading for the left-hand end of Chearsley (hidden in the trees ahead). Go through the gate 220 yards ahead in the fence across your route and continue in the long field beyond, gradually moving to the right and converging on the River Thame, whose course through the meadows is lined by willows. Cross the Thame on a footbridge into the field below Chearsley church. From the footbridge head just to the right of the church and after 100 yards go through a kissing gate on the right and out into Church Lane.

Chearsley is another of the witchert villages, but it has fewer witchert structures than Haddenham. Instead the character of Chearsley is formed much more by its narrow sunken village roads which were worn into the hillside above the

River Thame in the days before the advent of modern road metalling.

The village has, in fact, moved its site, for it originally lay between the church and the River Thame. The population of that earlier settlement was wiped out by the Black Death in 1348 and when new inhabitants began to farm the village's fields they abandoned the old site and built anew on the present site, out of reach of the Thame's floodwaters.

The church nave and chancel date from the thirteenth century.

Go up Church Lane, passing a length of witchert wall on the right, then the church on the left. At the point where Shupps Lane diverges right from Church Lane, turn left, climb the beaten earth path up the bank, and go over a stile into the field above the church. Bear slightly to the right across the field, aiming for the gate visible in the hedge ahead and crossing a fenced farm track which runs in front of the gate. Once over the stile beside the gate continue in the same direction through two fields along a well-defined path with a fence along its right-hand side. Soon the pyramid roof of Notley Dovecote comes into view, dead ahead on the next hill.

Cross the London–Banbury railway and carry straight on downhill beside the fence on your left, to go through the gateway in the corner ahead. In front of you now a stream skirts a wood; bear very slightly right to walk, with the stream a few yards away on your left, through a small plantation of trees until, in about 100 yards, you are able to cross the stream by a footbridge.

From the other side of the bridge head *very* slightly left across a small field to a stile which was built using an adjacent willow for one upright (just to the left of a gate). Then bearing left, go uphill to cross the section of wooden fencing at the left-hand end of the wire fence across the top of the field. Once over the fencing walk uphill to the skyline beside the patchy field boundary on your left, flanked by an overhead electricity line on the right. Gradually the great bulk of Notley Dovecote appears over the skyline ahead on the left.

The Dovecote, built in the 14th or 15th centuries to provide food for the monks of Notley Abbey, was renovated in 1971 by the Friends of the Vale of Aylesbury. It is only open to the public on certain autumn Sundays.

Once over the summit a farm appears ahead. As you reach it bear right to skirt behind the barn and silos. Climb the stile in the field corner beside the electricity line pole to reach the farm track running between you and the large intensive chicken-rearing building ahead. Turn left to follow this fenced farm track downhill into the valley, leaving the farm*house* on your left.

On the left, down in the valley, can be seen the roofs of Notley Abbey. Founded in 1161, the Abbey was occupied by Augustinian Canons who lived under severe rule, observing a vow of silence (except for worship). The Augustinians were evicted and much of the Abbey destroyed in 1538 after which the surviving buildings became a farm. Further demolitions and rebuildings took place in later centuries, but even so, large parts of the present house's walls once formed part of the Abbey.

Just over 100 yards beyond the farmhouse, on reaching the gate across the track, climb the stile immediately to right of the gate and maintain your course, now on a fenced footpath running beside the track (which has become the drive from Notley Abbey). After passing the buildings of the Abbey the path curves and ends at a stile into the field on right. Climb the stile and, with your back to the Abbey, cross the field to a stile in the fence opposite. Go over this and another immediately beyond it to continue ahead along the left-hand (bottom) side of a large sloping field; a mill stream fed by the River Thame is winding in the trees beside you. Go through the gate in the corner ahead and turn left to cross the bridge over the water roaring through the millraces of the former Notley Mill.

While pausing to look at the few pieces of brickwork surviving in the undergrowth around the millraces, it is interesting to reflect that, well into this century, a substantial brick-built water mill (Notley Mill) stood here, together with the miller's house, warehouses, and outbuildings. This was the last of a succession of mills which had ground corn on this site for centuries.

Once over the millraces, turn sharp left along the raised earth bank beside the mill stream for 150 yards, then turn right, and cross the River Thame by footbridge. Now bear left at 11 o'clock across the field to the far left-hand corner by the end of a small wood known as Crosse's Covert. Go over the stile into the right-hand of the two fields ahead, and walk up the left-hand side of the field; at its top go through the gateway and straight on uphill on a mid-field track to cross the A418 road.

Go through the gap in the hedge on the opposite side of the A418. Then, with the road squarely behind you cross the middle of the field, aiming for a solitary tree seen immediately to the left of a group of six silver farm silos in the middle distance. Continue in this direction until you come to the Haddenham–Thame road through a gap in the hedge.

Turn left along the road for 200 yards, then right, through the next gateway on the right (beside an under-road culvert with handrails). Now go diagonally left across two fields, aiming (in the begining of the first field) just to the right of the point on the skyline where the left-hand end of the Chiltern escarpment dips out of view. (Fix your course across the first field before leaving the gateway because the aiming point soon disappears.) These two fields are separated by a bridleway flanked by a fence with a stile in it. Climb the stile and continue the same course in the second field, aiming just to the left of a short row of trees visible on the middle skyline in front of the Chilterns. This course converges on Station Road, which you join by crossing a stile beside a farm gate. Turn right along the road into Haddenham until you reach Church End Green.

Haddenham has many buildings of historic or architectural interest but perhaps the most distinctive is the timber-framed Church Farm House, standing on the left of the church. Details of it are given on page 29.

Now turn left along Churchway, and first left along a footpath called Dragon Tail (it starts almost opposite the Green Dragon public house and runs between witchert walls). At the end of the footpath (in Skittles Green) turn right along the road (Gibson Lane). In a few yards, on reaching a "T" junction, turn left into The Croft which quickly curves to the right. Opposite the first of a row of bungalows, turn left down Turnstile, another walled footpath and, at the end of it, turn right into High Street. Walk the length of High Street to return to the starting place, Fort End.

Far Horizons

Walk 11	6 miles
O.S. 1:25,000 scale map SP72 (Pathfinder Series 1070)	

NORTH MARSTON — PITCHCOTT — DENHAM — QUAINTON — WOAD HILL — NORTH MARSTON

Starting point: North Marston Village Green outside The Bell public house (Grid ref: 775227)

This walk is best undertaken on a fine day with good visibility. It crosses the summits of Pitchcott and Woad Hills (both over 500 ft) from which views of over 15 miles into neighbouring counties can be enjoyed. Take an O.S. Landranger map with you to pick out the more distant landmarks. Another reason for choosing a fine day is that there is very little shelter on the way!

Travel

The streets of North Marston are generally narrow and unsuitable for parking. With care, however, parking places can be found which do not cause obstruction; the lay-by on School Hill in front of the school (on north side of churchyard) is one such place.

For bus users, Red Rover route 2 (Aylesbury–Winslow–Buckingham) and Aylesbury Bus route 66 (Aylesbury–Winslow–Buckingham–Akeley) combine to give a weekday service which averages *one per hour. There are no Sunday buses.*

Refreshments

In North Marston there is a pub but there is no longer any food shop. Quainton has several public houses scattered around the village and a grocery shop in Church Street, near the village green.

Route

Starting with The Bell public house on your left, set off along the unusually narrow High Street, leaving a large red-brick antique shop on your right. Ignore School Hill on left and continue ahead on a metalled footpath to converge on another road and quickly turn right into Schorne Lane. Bear left when Morton Close goes off on right at the Methodist Church, and soon left again when the road forks beside a water pump.

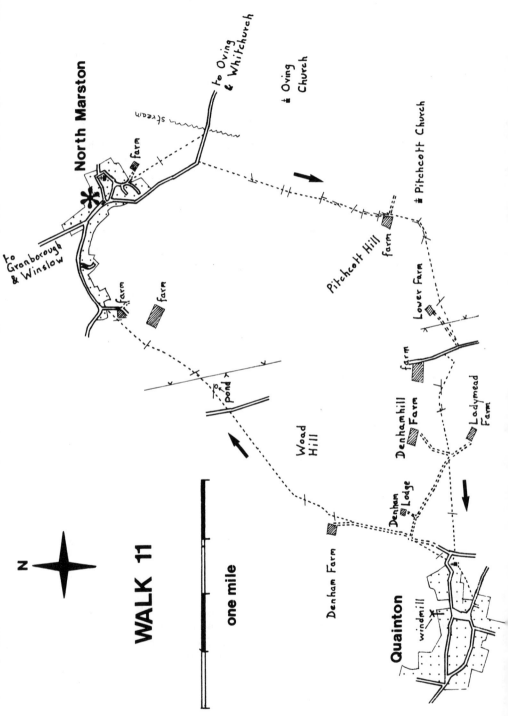

WALK 11

N

one mile

North Marston

to Oving & Whitchurch

stream

farm

to Granborough & Winslow

farm

farm

☩ Oving Church

☩ Pitchcott Church

Pitchcott Hill farm

Lower Farm

farm

Denhamhill Farm

Ladymead Farm

pond

Woad Hill

Denham Lodge

Denham Farm

Quainton

windmill

58

The raised rectangular cover beside the pump conceals John Schorne's well. Schorne, rector of North Marston from 1290 to 1314, developed a reputation for piety. He blessed the well here, after which its waters apparently took on healing powers and became used by physicians in Aylesbury and Winslow to make up medicines for eye diseases, gout, and rheumatism. After his death his shrine in North Marston parish church became a place of pilgrimage for sufferers from these complaints on such a scale that the authorities moved it to St. George's Chapel, Windsor, in 1478. People have tasted the waters in recent years but, ironically, it has lately been found necessary to suspend the practice on health grounds.

30 yards beyond Schorne's well go over the stile on right immediately in front of a gate across the track to enter the first field. Diverge very slightly to right of the curving course of the track you have just left and cross the field to climb the broad section of fencing in the hedge ahead. Maintain the same course across the next field, aiming slightly to left of the tower of Oving church (visible amongst trees on the skyline). This course converges on the right-hand hedge, 50 yards before the corner of the field; climb the stile to come out on to the Oving–North Marston road.

Turn right along the road. Leave it through the field gate on the left *at the beginning* of the first bend in the road. Now set off gently uphill beside the hedge along the right-hand side of the field. Go through the gate ahead in the corner (beside a small barn) and resume your course beside the hedge on right, soon beginning to drop downhill in the next field. Just before reaching the next hedge ahead move a few yards to left to cross the stile in the fence across your path; then cross a narrow strip of pasture to go over the pair of stiles in the hedge in front of you.

With the pair of stiles squarely behind you head at between 11 and 12 o'clock across the next field to cross the stile a little left of centre in the hedge ahead (ignore the gate on left in the same hedge). Maintain the same course for 120 yards along the left-hand side of the following field, then cross the horse jump on left where the hedge gives way to a fence. Once over the jump, take care to resume your previous course, diverging slowly from the fence on right.

While crossing this field it is worth stopping to turn around and take in the panoramic view behind you. The water tower rising above the skyline is at Mursley, about 6 miles away, between Winslow and Milton Keynes; due to its height and colour it is a landmark for ramblers all over North Bucks. Closer at hand, the picture-book village of Oving tops the nearest hill.

Go through a gap in the hedge ahead, and straight across a narrow neck of field beyond, to a small gate in the hedge on the far side. Continue in the same direction beyond the gate, now nearly at the summit of Pitchcott Hill and walking beside the fence on the left towards the large barn on the skyline. Go through the gate in front of the barn, bear left to go through the gate at the barn corner, then maintain the same course across a small paddock and leave it through a gate in the fence/hedge ahead.

In the superb view from this gate the skyline is the Chiltern escarpment, and the "small" detached hill on it is Ivinghoe Beacon, about 12 miles to south-east.

Now turn right to go through the small gate in the nearby corner, cross the road leading to the farmhouse, and continue ahead beside the hedge/fence on right, leaving the farmhouse on your right. The fence soon turns away to right, whereupon leave it and maintain your course down the field to reach the right-hand corner ahead and go through the gateway in the fence in front of you.

On the left, across the field, are the roofs of the hamlet of Pitchcott. The church is no longer used for worship and has been beautifully converted into a house. Looking ahead, the low foreground ridge of hills rises to the right to the tree-clad Lodge Hill on which the pinnacles of Waddesdon Manor can just be seen on the summit amidst the trees. The skyline range of hills is again the Chiltern escarpment; rising above it you may make out the 320 ft-high telecommunication relay tower at Stokenchurch, about 14 miles to the south.

Once through the gateway bear right to follow the right-hand hedge downhill. When it turns to left, go over the stile* in the corner into the upper corner of the next field. Drop downhill diagonally across the field, to go through the gate in the bottom hedge a little to the left of the buildings of Lower Farm. On across the following field, passing beneath the pylon line, to the far right-hand corner. Go through the field gate and turn left for a few paces to reach and turn right along the road.

This lonely road has seen a lot of history. It was a minor Roman road, linking the great imperial artery of Akeman Street (at Fleet Marston) to the walled Roman town of Towcester, on Watling Street. In mediaeval times it was part of the main road from London through Aylesbury to Buckingham. During the turnpike era it was superseded by

---

*Stile needed and installation requested in 1988.

the modern A413, running a few miles to the east on higher, drier ground. Since then it has been left alone with its memories, but if the A413 route had not been developed you certainly would not be walking down the middle of this road now.

After 110 yards along the road, leave it by crossing the stile in the left-hand hedge into the left-hand corner of a field (it is located immediately beyond the gate into the previous field). Follow the left-hand hedge for about 70 yards until it bends slightly to the left (just before it goes beneath an overhead electricity line). At this point turn right and cross the field to the nearest point in the hedge on the right (seen just below the buildings of Denhamhill Farm on the hillside beyond). The nearest point turns out to be a corner in the hedge where the wire fence on the right joins it. Go through the gate in the hedge 20 yards to the left of the corner and immediately turn left to walk beside the hedge along the left-hand margin of the next field. Continue through the gate in the hedge ahead and straight on across the following field to pass close on the right side of the first electricity pole from the twin-poled overhead electricity line post.

Leave the field in the far left-hand corner through the gateway with cattle grid used by the track coming down from Denhamhill Farm. Turn right along the access road beyond and immediately go through another gateway with cattle grid. Now leave the road and bear left at between 10 and 11 o'clock across the field, aiming just to left of Quainton's windmill, whose top half is visible on the skyline. Go over the stile in the middle of the wire fence across your path and maintain the same course across the next field to come down to a roadside stile at the left-hand end of the railings which surround a small stone-built pumping station (not visible until over summit).

Go through the kissing gate on the opposite side of the road and up through the churchyard, turning at the top to follow the path round the left side of the church. Just beyond the south porch turn left to go out into a field through another kissing gate. Cross the top of the field to climb the nearby stile in the right-hand hedge and continue downhill along a fenced footpath. At the end of the fenced section cross the stile and continue along the side of a small paddock to reach the road at the corner of the timber-framed house ahead. Turn right along the road and right again after 100 yards to walk up the side of Quainton's village green.

For notes on Quainton and its windmill please see the beginning of walk no. 4, "The Quainton Hills".

At the head of the green turn right to follow Church Street. After passing the historic Winwood Almshouses stay on the road as it curves left past the church; leave it at the bottom of the hill by turning left over the stile beside a gate (opposite a disused building with Victorian brick upper works over much older stone lower parts). Go uphill across the field and climb the stile in the hedge ahead. Continue ahead in the following field to pass close to the corner of the garden on right and to slowly converge on the road on right to join it in the far right-hand corner of the field.

The distinctive waymarks featuring a horseshoe, which can be seen on a post where you join the road, indicate that you are crossing the Swan's Way, a 65 mile-long bridleway route from Goring-on-Thames to Salcey Forest in Northampton-shire.

Immediately beyond the field corner the road forks. Take the left-hand road and follow it towards the two houses.

Before reaching the houses look right to see Denham Lodge, a seventeenth-century house with an older core standing (partly hidden by trees) on the island within a moat. Although moated sites were once fairly common settings for the houses of the local gentry (see page 127) it is rare to find one still occupied. Another unusual feature is that Denham Lodge had its own deer park. It was on the hillside behind the moat, enclosed by a brick wall which can be seen running up the hillside and over the skyline. The course of the encircling wall is still complete, although it is now in a rather ruinous and patched condition.

Continue uphill beyond the houses until the road begins to curve left to Denham Farm. Leave it here and bear very slightly right uphill, passing obliquely beneath the telegraph line to go over the stile to right of the farm gate in the fence/hedge which runs *across* the hill ahead. Next bear right between 1 and 2 o'clock over the ridge ahead to cross the stile in the fence which becomes visible ahead on the same ridge. (The stile is located near a gate just above the point where the fence gives way to a hedge, in a valley over to the right.)

Once over the stile, maintain the same course and climb to the summit ahead. The summit is reached at the point where a short, grassy holloway comes up from the right. As the flat summit of the hill is breasted, the village of North Marston appears ahead in the valley, with Oving on the hill to its right. Aiming at the left-hand end of North Marston, carry on over the summit and downhill to come out on to the road through the five-bar gate seen almost midway between two pylons visible beyond it.

Cross the road and enter the next field via the gate opposite. Cross this field diagonally to the left, and leave it over a stile set in the left-hand hedge just before a pond (ringed by trees) is reached. With your back to the stile, aim diagonally at between 1 and 2 o'clock across the next field, pass beneath the pylon line and go through a small gate in the hedge on right (it is the second gateway in this hedge, counting from the pond). Uphill in the following field, diverging slowly from the right-hand hedge to go through the gate in the middle of the hedge ahead (not visible until you are over the summit). Straight ahead along the middle of the ensuing field, keeping 20 yards out from the point of the hedge projecting into the field from right, to go through the fence ahead via the gate immediately to left of the farm barns. Leaving the farm to right cross the final small paddock diagonally to the far left corner, climb the stile there, and turn left along the narrow road. After a few yards, at the road junction, turn right to follow the road back into North Marston.

The Hill Walk

Walk 12	7¾ miles
O.S. 1:25,000 scale maps SP61, 71	
(Pathfinder Series 1093)	

BRILL — CHILTON — ASHENDON — DORTON — BRILL

Starting point: Brill Parish Church (Grid ref: 656138)

Anyone who believes that Buckinghamshire north of the Chilterns is flat will revise their opinion after completing this circuit. It runs through three of the villages perched on steep-sided hills formed by the survival of small pockets of hard Portland stone. As a result, in under 8 miles this route descends a total of 770 feet and, because it is circular, it climbs the same height. Undertaken at a steady pace this is perfect for toning up your muscles while enjoying a superb set of views.

Travel

Brill has no official car parks, but there are several places in which cars can be parked considerately on street.

Bus travellers are confined to a very sparse service from Aylesbury on Wednesdays and Saturdays (Heyfordian) and from Oxford on Fridays and Saturdays (Motts). In view of the infrequency of these services they cannot be recommended as a convenient means of starting and ending the day.

Refreshments

Brill has grocery shops in High Street and Temple Street and also several pubs. Ashendon has a pub, and sweets etc. can be bought at the Post Office/ Grocery behind the pub. Chilton and Dorton have no pubs or shops.

Route

Start at the green on the south side of Brill parish church. Leaving the church on your left go to the east end of the green and, bearing right, cross the stile between houses nos. 13 and 15. Set off along the well-worn path beyond, which takes you across the head of a valley; then climb the stile beside the gate ahead. Maintain the same course for 100 yards in the next field, walking beside the hedge/fence on your left, then turn left through the first gate reached and continue at a right angle to your previous course, walking beside the fence/hedge on your left. Cross the stile in the corner ahead.

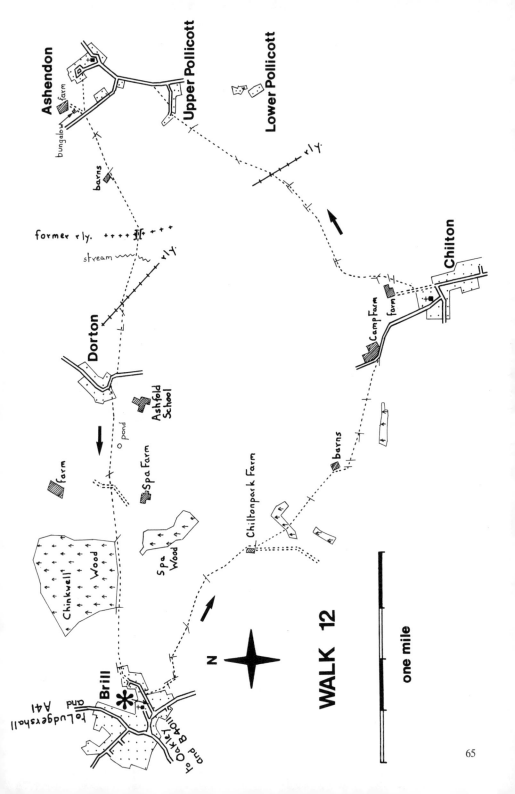

Ashendon

bungalow farm

Upper Pollicott

Lower Pollicott

barns

former rly. + + + + + + +

stream

rly.

rly.

Dorton

Chilton

Camp Farm

farm

Ashfold School

pond

barns

farm

Spa Farm

Chiltonpark Farm

Chinkwell Wood

Spa Wood

N

WALK 12

Brill

to Ludgershall A41 and

to Oakley and B4011

one mile

65

With the Vale of Aylesbury laid out in front of you bear diagonally right downhill across the next field, aiming at between 1 and 2 o'clock, and soon leaving an electricity line pole to your left. As you descend the hill a line of twin electricity poles is converging on your left. Your next goal is the gate beside the furthest of these twin poles and to reach it you cross a stile in the wire fence* across the hillside and continue along the top of the broad ridge in the field beyond. On reaching the gate, climb the stile beside it and change direction slightly to the right to climb and pass close to the left-hand end of the buildings of Chiltonpark Farm, on their lonely hilltop. On rounding the corner of the barns bear slightly right to walk along the side of the farm, over the summit, and down to go through the gate in the fence ahead.

Now bear left downhill, aiming at 11 o'clock to reach the mid-point of the bottom field boundary where (in 1988) there was a gap between a thin line of poplars and a thicker row of mixed trees. Cross the stiles and footbridge into this gap, walk through the narrow tree belt, and cross another footbridge and stile. Now on the level, continue straight ahead across the middle of the following field (aiming at the nearest of two barns which soon become visible ahead in the next field).

In January–February 1984 this remote countryside became the focus of national attention when a sea eagle strayed widely from its northern habitat and settled in the small pieces of woodland around you. The nation's birdwatchers descended on the area, armed with binoculars and telescopes, to line the local roads as they waited patiently for a sight of the wanderer. After a stay of about two weeks, when the local farmers were beginning to fear for the safety of their new lambs, the sea eagle took off and vanished as mysteriously as it had arrived.

Cross the stiles and footbridges in the fence/hedge ahead, then maintain your course across the ensuing field, now aiming at the further barn, to meet the left-hand hedge boundary at a projecting corner just before the barns are reached. From the corner continue ahead along the edge of the field past both barns (the remains of Chilton Grove Farm) and turn left over a stile 50 yards further on. Cross the narrow belt of young oak trees, then two more stiles in quick succession, and continue on the level across the following field to the far right-hand corner.

Cross the footbridge in the corner and head uphill, aiming a little to the right, to cross the fence ahead near its mid-point (just left of a hollow in the hillside and 130 yards from the upper right-hand corner). Continue diagonally right uphill across the next field to a kissing gate in the top right-hand corner

*Not visible until you are nearly upon it.

(opposite Camp Farm) which brings you to a road. Turn right and follow the road into the village of Chilton.

In its commanding hilltop position, Chilton is all that the traditional English village is held to be — quiet, attractive, and timeless. The parish church, with its interesting collection of monuments, typifies the continuous building and rebuilding which has created the character of our churches — it has a thirteenth-century chancel, a fourteenth-century tower, a fifteenth-century nave and a sixteenth-century south chapel.

Turn left at the "T" junction in the centre of Chilton, and in a few yards, when the road swings sharp right, turn left again through a gateway to follow a private drive.

On your left is the imposing Chilton House, and on your right, across the valley, your next objective — the left-hand one of the two hamlets of Pollicott.

Chilton House, built in 1740 for Lord Chief Justice Carter, was modelled on Buckingham House in London. The latter was subsequently acquired by George III and became the (now hidden) core of Buckingham Palace. Today Chilton House is a home for the elderly; one can only envy them the views from their windows.

Continue past the House and its outbuildings. Thirty yards beyond the last outbuilding (a stone-built barn) leave the track, and cross the stile into the field on your right. From the stile bear left,* aiming for the twin-pole electricity line post seen on the next ridge just to the right of the farm barns. As you come over the brow of the hill bear slightly right to aim for a stile in the fence along the bottom of the valley, then for another, in the fence beyond it (beside a single electricity line pole). Change direction to left uphill from the second stile to the right-hand of two gates near to the twin electricity pole mentioned above.

Once through the gate turn left and walk beside the hedge on your left, first across the top of the field, then turning to go down the left-hand side of this and two following fields to the flat valley bottom. (At the bottom of the first field take care to cross the stiles and footbridge immediately to the right of the corner in order to stay on the path.) At the bottom of the third of these fields cross the footbridge in the left-hand corner and continue in the same direction, now beside a fence on your right, to cross the Marylebone–Banbury railway.

*During the next 600 yards the route described gradually veers to as much as 100 yards to the west of the legal line of this path. The reason for this is that the next two stiles and gate have unfortunately been sited off the legal route.

On the far side of the railway bear half left (aiming a little to the left of the left-hand hamlet on the skyline — Upper Pollicott) and cross the lower end of this huge field diagonally to a gate in the hedge ahead (not visible until you are half way across the field). Once through the gate turn right and walk up the field, over the right-hand shoulder of the small hill ahead, and into a farmyard in Upper Pollicott through the field gate immediately to the right of the nearest house. (Shortly before reaching the hamlet you pass through the left-hand of two gates in a fence across the field).

Turn right to leave the farmyard and continue along the road for about 90 yards. Opposite the far end of the first row of cottages on the right, turn left through a small gate, then over a stile into the field beyond. Go straight ahead uphill across the field, quickly passing beneath an overhead power line and leaving the nearest pole 15 yards to your left. Cross the stile in the hedge/fence ahead and turn left to walk along the road into Ashendon. Turn second left (at the church) and walk down the road to the Red Lion public house.

The windswept village of Ashendon clings to its limestone-capped hilltop above the Vale, with views in all directions from it. The tiny church, most of which dates from the thirteenth century or earlier, seems to huddle from the elements in its exposed position. On clear days, as you walk down the road to the Red Lion, you have a superb view northward across the lower slopes of the Cotswolds towards Northants. The line of tall chimney stacks is 6 miles away at the Calvert brickworks, south of Buckingham.

Turn left in front of the Red Lion and follow the footpath between the two houses opposite. On reaching the field bear slightly right to cross it to a gate in the far boundary (a little to the left of the bungalow).

The cluster of industrial buildings in the panorama below you on the right is the Royal Ordnance Research and Development Centre at Westcott, on the site of a former RAF airfield. See page 17 for further details.

Go through the gate, cross the road, and over the fence *directly* opposite. With Dorton village ahead, nestling in the valley below Brill Hill, diverge from the fence on your left and head downhill, aiming at between 12 and 1 o'clock, to a stile/footbridge in the hedge ahead (not visible until you are over the brow of the hill).

On the right, in the trees below, can be seen Wotton church with the eighteenth-century Wotton House (one-time home of the Dukes of Buckingham) to the left of it. Walk no. 3 gives you a closer view of these.

Continue the same diagonal course across the middle of the next field, going over a shoulder of the hill and diverging at about 1 o'clock from the hedge on your left. Leave this field through a gap in the hedge ahead, a few yards uphill from a group of barns (which do not become visible until you are over the shoulder of the hill). Once through the gap, turn right to the corner, then left to continue down the lower side of the field, walking beside the hedge on your right.

Just before the bottom right-hand corner of the field, bear right through a gateway and up over a farm access bridge which spans the trackbed of the former railway from Ashendon Junction to Grendon Underwood Junction. (Named expresses between London and Yorkshire once thundered beneath this bridge.) At the far end of the bridge ramp go through the gate and straight ahead across the field to cross a stream using the footbridge in front of you. Then on across the next field to its far left-hand corner. Here turn left over the stile to recross the Marylebone–Banbury railway.

From the far side of the railway bear right and, after 30 yards, pass through a gap in the hedge on the right side of the field, then bear left across the corner of the following field to go through the small gate in the left-hand hedge. With the village of Dorton now visible on the right, continue in the same direction across the next field to go over a stile on to the road ahead. (The stile is directly in front of the lodge house for Ashfold School in the trees ahead, and is just to the right of a field gate.)

Ashfold School, seen to the left of its lodge, occupies Dorton House, a large Jacobean mansion standing in wooded parkland.

Turn right for 130 yards along the road into Dorton. Follow it as it curves left, then, as it swings sharp right, leave it and take to the metalled footpath which goes off on the left immediately before the entrance to Brook Farm. Follow this path, with a stream on your right at first, until it ends at a stile leading into a field. (Ignore the path branching left just after a footbridge.)

Pause at the stile to get your bearings. You can see the houses of Brill ahead on the skyline and, immediately to right of them, Chinkwell Wood covering the hillside. Shortly you will be walking up the left-hand margin of that wood.

Set off from the stile to cross three fields in a generally straight line, aiming for the bottom left-hand corner of Chinkwell Wood. In the first field you quickly pass beneath one overhead electricity line, while another, at a right angle to it, diverges gently to your left; a midfield pond (marked by three trees) is 15 yards to your left. Go over a stile in the fence on the far side of this field and continue across the next two fields aiming straight to the bottom left-hand corner of the wood. (The boundary between these latter two fields is a fenced farm track with stiles on both sides, near a field gate.) Hidden from sight until you reach it on the far side of the third field is a small gate at the corner of the wood; the gate leads into the large field sloping uphill. Go through the gate, turn right, and walk uphill along the edge of the wood.

As you start the climb, look across to your left to Spa Wood, on the other side of the field. The trees there hide the site of Dorton Spa, which was developed in the 1830's around a medicinal spring for which considerable healing powers were claimed. Various spa buildings were put up, a 12-acre park (the site of the present wood) laid out, and entertainment consisting of billiards, reading rooms and a ballroom was provided. Dorton was all set to become one of the growing number of English spas. A spa hotel opened in Brill and visitors drove down a track across this field to take the foul-tasting waters (which contained an unusually high proportion of iron sulphate). After a modest start, however, the sheer inaccessibility of the spa killed it and it closed after less than 20 years of operation. (The railway to Dorton, which might have brought customers, was not built until half a century after the spa closed.) The spa buildings fell into decay, trees covered the park, and now all that remains are the footings of the former buildings and a small brick hut over the spring. (There is no public access to the wood.)

At the top corner of the field (and the wood) go through the small gate in the fence ahead and continue uphill beside the fence on your right.

The two lines of new trees, interspersed with the stumps of old ones, mark the site of the grand avenue from Brill down to the Spa.

Go through the gate in the top right-hand corner of this last field and ahead on the unmade track along the edge of a housing estate. This brings you on to a residential road in Brill. Follow this back to the green.

Going
Great Western

PRINCES RISBOROUGH — HORSENDEN — BLEDLOW — ILMER — PRINCES RISBOROUGH

Starting point: Princes Risborough Parish Church (Grid ref: 805034)

Much of this walk has as a backdrop the impressive northern edge of the Chiltern Hills. The route will appeal to railway lovers, since, in a little over eight miles, it encounters four different railway lines radiating from the junction at Princes Risborough. Until a few years ago, the walker on this circuit would hardly ever have been out of ear-shot of railway activity, but today things are much quieter since two of the lines (to Chinnor and Thame) now carry freight only.

Travel

For motorists The Mount public car park in Stratton Road behind Princes Risborough parish church provides ample space.

For public transport travellers there is a daily train service between London (Marylebone), High Wycombe and Princes Risborough at roughly hourly intervals (2-hourly on Sundays). On weekdays there is a train service between Princes Risborough and Aylesbury at roughly 2-hourly intervals.

Bee Line bus services 323/4 (Aylesbury–Princes Risborough–High Wycombe) run every 30 minutes on weekdays and every two hours on Sundays. Alight from buses in Princes Risborough Market Place.

Refreshments

In Princes Risborough there is a variety of shops and pubs in High Street, Duke Street and Bell Street. At Bledlow there is The Lions public house, but Horsenden and Ilmer offer no eating or drinking facilities.

Route

Princes Risborough is a pleasant ancient market town on the Neolithic route from Norfolk to Wiltshire known as the Icknield Way; today, fortunately, a relief road leaves the High Street dominated by pedestrians. The town's great mediaeval feature, the Castle of the Black Prince, has long since

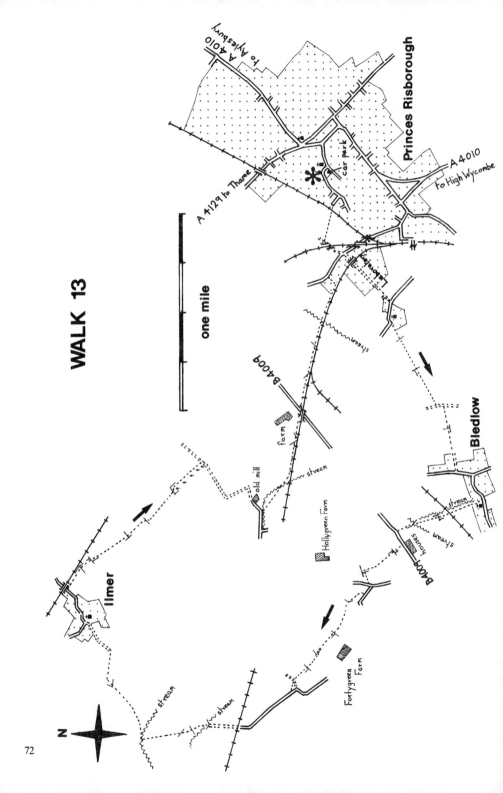

WALK 13

one mile

N

vanished and its site is occupied today by The Mount car park beside the parish church. Later centuries have, however, left fine buildings such as the seventeenth-century Manor House just east of the church, the fifteenth-century Old Vicarage just north of the church, and the Town Hall, built in 1824 in the Market Place, with its first-floor Council Chamber supported on stilts above an area which is used as a market to this day.

Rail travellers turn left at the end of the station approach road, and follow Summerleys Road under the railway bridges to reach the Princes Risborough Laboratory. Turn left there, and jump one paragraph in this text.

Motorists and bus travellers start this walk in Stratton Road between the west end of Princes Risborough's parish church, and The Mount public car park. Set off westward, along Stratton Road leaving the car park on your left. Turn down the second road on the right (Mount Way); at the head of this cul-de-sac take to a path and follow it across the Aylesbury branch railway line into a field. Maintain the same course across the field aiming slightly right of a bridge beneath the main line to Banbury. Just before reaching the bridge turn left on to an access track and follow it beneath the bridge, and on past a former water mill to a road junction.

Cross over the main road and follow the access road opposite (which is sign-boarded to Princes Risborough Laboratory) as it goes under another railway bridge (the Chinnor and Thame branches this time).

The Princes Risborough Laboratory, which was opened in 1925, has carried out much valuable research work on the use of timber in the building industry. Its work on wood preservatives, for example, has led to changes in modern building practices which have greatly extended the likely life of timber used in window frames. Regrettably this establishment is likely to close during the currency of this book.

Continue straight ahead along the access road between the Laboratory buildings and go over a stile at the end of the road; maintain the same course along the right-hand side of a field, then cross the stiles ahead in and out of a farmyard, and so to the road in the hamlet of Horsenden.

Horsenden Manor was built in 1810 on the site of a much older building. The small church is actually the chancel of an earlier building whose nave was demolished in 1765, whereupon the redundant stone was used to build the present tower. Both the church and the original house were once enclosed by a moat but only part of its earthworks survive today. In 1820 and 1900 weapons from the Civil War period were found in

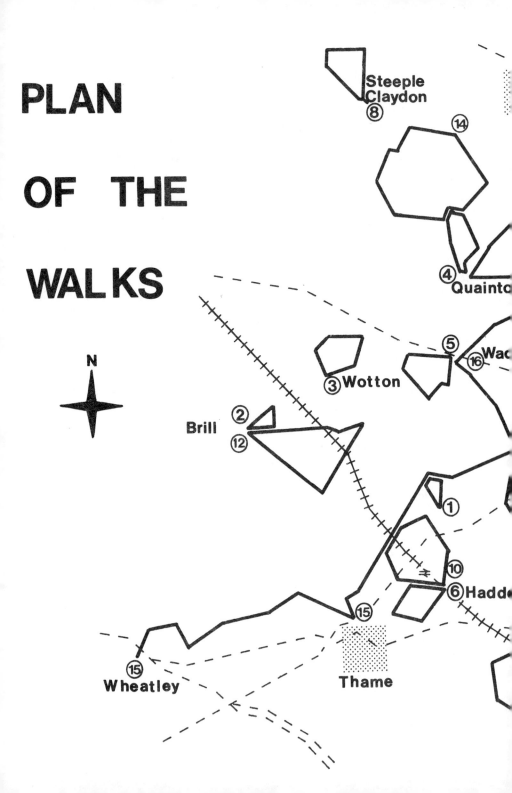

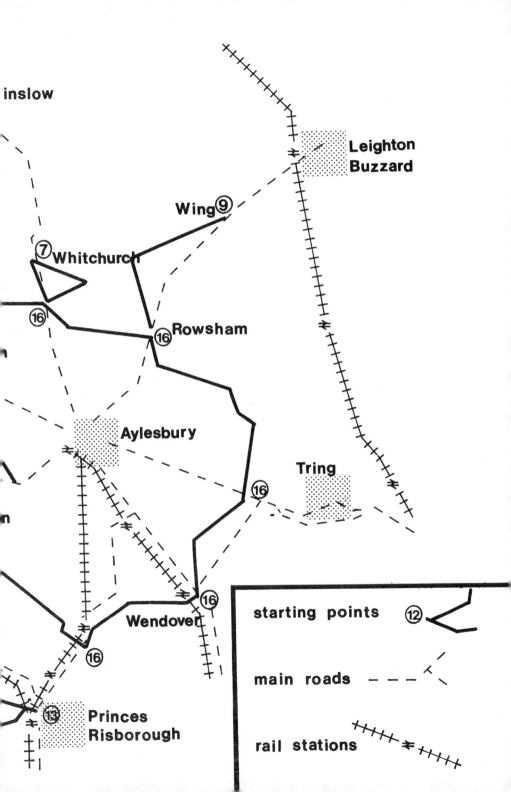

inslow

Leighton
Buzzard

Wing ⑨

⑦ Whitchurch

⑯

⑯ Rowsham

Aylesbury

Tring

⑯

⑯

Wendover

⑯

⑬ Princes
Risborough

starting points ⑫

main roads — — —

rail stations

the moat, and it is thought that the old house was garrisoned for the King by the owner at that time — Sir John Denham.

In Horsenden turn right to follow the road past Horsenden Manor (on left) and the church. When the road swings sharp right beside a pond (at the entrance to Manor Farm), leave it by going straight ahead through a gate (opposite the pond) to enter a field. Follow the fence/hedge on the left until it turns away, after which maintain your course across the field to go over the stile in the hedge ahead. Then maintain the same course across the middle of the field beyond and beside the right-hand hedge of the following field.

At the far end of the latter field follow the path as it turns left to run through a thicket along the route of an abandoned road; after 60 yards turn right and climb a stile into a field and then continue beside the left-hand hedge of this field and the next. Go through the gate ahead and along the track past the sheds to come out on to a road. Turn left and walk up the road to a "T" junction; here turn right along Church End to reach Bledlow church, where you leave the road through the first entrance into the churchyard.

Bledlow's church (dating from Norman times) is situated on the edge of a steep-sided wooded valley from which flows the Lyde brook. The brook was formerly dammed at a number of points here to create watercress beds in the clear spring water. Most of these have now been abandoned and the section of the Lyde's valley beside the church has been turned into a most attractive garden by Lord Carrington, who lives at the Manor House near the church.

Follow the footpath through the churchyard (passing close by the east end of the chancel) and then on downhill with a steep drop into the valley of the Lyde on the right (the newly-created garden is visible from the path). Pass the solitary house on the right and continue straight ahead through its garden, then down the middle of the field beyond, to cross the Chinnor branch railway.

This railway originally ran from Princes Risborough to Watlington. Traffic on it was never substantial, and passenger services were withdrawn in 1957. In 1961 the line was closed completely between Chinnor and Watlington and the only surviving freight traffic on it runs to the cement works at Chinnor.

Maintain the same direction down the field beyond the railway, and when the field twists to the right, leave it by going through the kissing gate straight ahead. Continue downhill beside the right-hand hedge in the next field. 50 yards after crossing over a stream bear right through a kissing gate in the hedge and then turn to follow the left-hand hedge of the neighbouring field to reach the road beside the red-roofed house.

Turn left along the road (the Lower Icknield Way, more prosaically known as B4009) for some 130 yards and then turn right through a kissing gate into a field (partially in allotments) opposite the first of a row of houses. Set off at a right angle to the road, walking beside the hedge on the left, cross the stile in the corner, and maintain the same direction across the curving field beyond to reach its far left-hand corner; turn left over the stile in the corner and follow the right-hand hedge of the next field to a road.

Turn left along the road for a few paces to reach a road junction at which turn right. About 80 yards along the second road turn right over a stile located immediately before the third house from the junction (The Willows). Follow the curving garden boundary of The Willows for about 50 yards to its outermost point, then bear left across the corner of the field to climb the stile in the hedge ahead, located some 10 yards from the right-hand end of a short row of willows. (While crossing the corner of this field the group of black-painted barns of Holly Green Farm should be two fields away on the right.)

Now go straight ahead along the edge of two fields, beside a wire fence on your right in the first field, and a hedge on your left in the second. (The buildings of Forty Green Farm are soon one field away on the left.) In the far corner of the second field go through the gate on the left, then turn right to resume your previous course along the edge of two more fields, beside a fence on the right in the first, and a hedge on the left in the second. In the far corner of the second field (the boundary steps out just before the real corner is reached) cross a hedged path by stiles. Now bear left along the cottage's rear garden boundary to reach the road via a stile. Turn right along the road and follow it for ⅓ mile to a level-crossing over the Thame branch railway.

This branch was once a through route between London, Princes Risborough and Oxford. Passenger services were withdrawn in 1963 and the line was closed altogether between Oxford and Thame in 1967. At Thame, however, is a regional oil distribution terminal and the surviving part of this branch between Risborough and Thame now carries a profitable traffic in bulk oil deliveries from refineries at Grain Island in Kent and Thames Haven in Essex.

Cross the line and continue for 250 yards along the green lane beyond. Go through the gate across the end of the lane and curve gradually to the left to cross the stile and footbridge in the hedge ahead (located 30 yards from the left-hand corner of the field).

From the footbridge bear right at between 1 and 2 o'clock across the field, to climb the stile in the hedge and maintain the same course across the ensuing field, going beneath an overhead electricity line en route, and passing midway between two of its poles. Cross the substantial footbridge over the stream which forms the northern edge of the field. Now bear right to cross the corner of the following field, passing beside the nearest double-pole telegraph post, to converge on the fence/hedge on the right and walk beside it to the corner of the field, heading towards the tiny spire of Ilmer church on the hill ahead. In the corner go through the gate ahead and turn right to walk along the left-hand side of a long narrow field. Leave by the second gate in the far left-hand corner and follow the green lane between hedges uphill into the hamlet of Ilmer, to emerge on the road beside the church.

The picturesque church in this diminutive village is basically twelfth-century, but its wooden spire was added in 1890.

Continue ahead along the road, past the church, through the village. Twenty yards before the railway bridge turn right through a small gate in the hedge to go along the left-hand side of two fields beside the railway line.

This railway, which is part of the route from London (Marylebone) via Princes Risborough to Banbury, was one of the last main lines to be built in this country. It was opened in 1906 to provide a short cut for the Great Western Railway's London–Birmingham services in place of their former route to Banbury via Reading and Oxford. It was downgraded to its present secondary status in 1966 when its former rival route from London (Euston) to Birmingham was electrified.

At the end of the second field pass through a gate and over a stream. On again through two fields, now beside a hedge on the right, gradually diverging from the railway. When, in the second field, the hedge turns away to the right, go straight across a small recessed corner of the field and through a gap in the hedge opposite; then turn right to the corner of the field, then left to follow the right-hand hedge to a copse ahead.

Follow the path through the long, narrow copse; at its far end ignore the green lane running to the left and turn right through a small gate in the hedge. Continue on a fenced path between fields at a right angle to the previous course and go through a gate in the hedge ahead. Stay on the fenced path as it turns sharp left and continues down the edge of the field. At the bottom of the field turn right on a track passing beside buildings of the former Bledlow paper mill. Beyond these the track becomes a road which bears right (beside a roadside barn) as it joins a stream; at this point cross the footbridge on the left over the stream. Now bear left and follow the sinuous left-hand boundary of the field (formed by the stream) until reaching the first gate on the left; go through the gate and over the stream, turn right and follow the stream to the Thame branch railway. Then turn left to follow the railway line along the right-hand side of three fields until a road is reached.

Cross the road to enter the field opposite and continue beside the railway along the right-hand margin of four fields into Princes Risborough.

On this section the distinctive shape of the Whiteleaf Cross becomes clearly visible carved out of the face of the Chiltern Hills ahead. There is no certainty about its origins; a Saxon boundary charter of A.D. 903 may refer to a predecessor of the present cross; the monks at Monks Risborough may have carved it; at the other extreme some hold it to be the work of Royalists during the Civil War. All that can be safely said is that it was well established by the early nineteenth century, at which time it began to receive official protection.

At the end of the fourth field carry on along the fenced path beside the railway. On the outskirts of the town the path turns left to run between gardens before emerging on to a road. On reaching the road turn right, and follow it until arriving at the entrance to Princes Risborough Laboratory (just before the road goes beneath a pair of railway bridges). At this point railway travellers should continue along the road under the bridges and turn right into the Station approach road. Other walkers should turn left down the road opposite to the Laboratory entrance and continue past the buildings of the old water mill. After passing under the railway arch bear to right off the track and cross the field diagonally towards the houses ahead (aiming for the right-hand end of the third house to the right of the church steeple). Cross the Aylesbury branch line and return to the car park via the outward route.

The Claydons

Walk 14	8½ miles
O.S. 1:25,000 scale map SP72	
(Pathfinder Series 1070)	

EAST CLAYDON — MIDDLE CLAYDON — FINEMEREHILL — HOGSHAW — EAST CLAYDON

Starting point: Road junction in middle of East Claydon (Grid ref: 737256)

Claydon House stands almost at the geographical centre of the pleasant quartet of villages known as The Claydons (East Claydon, Steeple Claydon, Middle Claydon and Botolph Claydon). This ramble passes through two of these villages and offers views towards the other two, as well as passing close by Claydon House, the family home of the Verneys for centuries. Much of the route is through countryside which was part of the Claydon Estate before it contracted to its modern boundaries.

Travel

Motorists should park in Church Way, East Claydon on the grass verge immediately beyond the end of the houses, where the road becomes a single-track lane. The area is served infrequently by Red Rover bus service 15 (Aylesbury–Calvert) on weekdays; there is no Sunday service.

Refreshments

The walk does not pass any pubs or shops. The nearest hostelries are at Steeple Claydon and Verney Junction, while the nearest shops can be found in Steeple Claydon and Winslow. If the time is right, however, you could sample the tea room at Claydon House; this is open from 2.30 to 5.30 p.m. (except Thursdays and Fridays) from April to October.

Route

Start the walk at the road junction in the middle of East Claydon village and set off along Sandhills Road, signposted to Steeple and Middle Claydon, Padbury and Buckingham. Leave the road through the gate on the left opposite the last of the row of nine modern houses and go straight ahead across the field to the left-hand (smaller) of the two gates in the far hedge (leave the pond 30 yards to your right and walk beside a short length of hedge on your right for the left few yards to the gate). Follow the right-hand

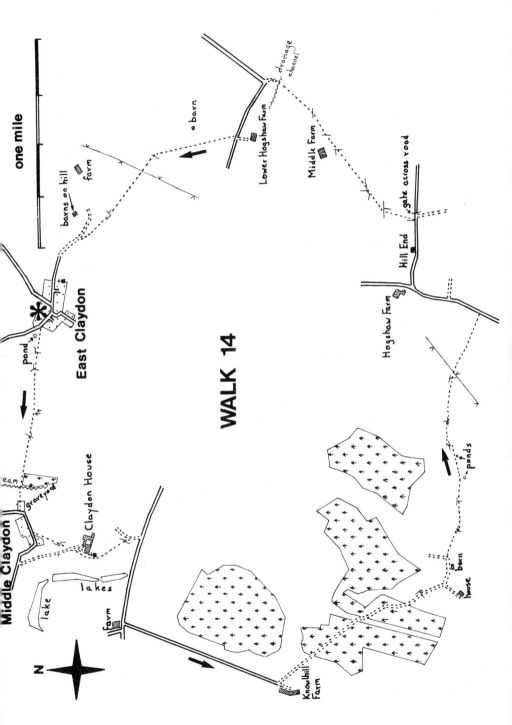

one mile

barns on hill
farm
a barn
drainage channel
Lower Hogshaw Farm
Middle Farm
gate across road
Hill End
Hogshaw Farm

East Claydon

pond

WALK 14

Claydon House
graveyard
stream
Middle Claydon
lake
lakes
farm

Knowlhill Farm

ponds
barn
house

N

81

hedge along the side of the next field, go through the gate in the corner ahead, and change direction very slightly to left across the middle of the field beyond, aiming (in 1988) for the right-hand edge of a small clump of trees standing on the far side of the field.

As you reach the tree clump a hedge comes in on your left and turns to run on in the direction in which you have been walking. Continue along the field edge, now on a gently falling gradient with the hedge on your left. Cross the fence in the corner ahead and maintain the same course beside the left-hand hedge of the two following fields (crossing a stream in the dip between them). In the second field, when an overhead electricity line crosses the path, go ahead over the footbridge and stile in front of you into a graveyard, to come out on to a road on the edge of the hamlet of Middle Claydon. Turn left and walk along the road for about 200 yards, then enter the field on the left through a gate immediately beyond the first house on the left.

> **This house is known as the Old Post Office but started life as a school and became the village library in about 1900. Today Middle Claydon has no school, post office or library, but the County Council send a mobile library round once a fortnight.**

Head across the field aiming at 1 o'clock towards Claydon House (part of which can be seen among the trees ahead), following a fence on your right. Before reaching the house go through the second gate in the fence (it is set at a right angle to the fence line). Now drop downhill, cross the drive at the point where it forks, and go through the kissing gate in the corner ahead at the point where the fence on the right meets the hedge which screens the house.

> **Pause at this gate to look to your right along the chain of artificial lakes formed by damming a tiny stream as it passes Claydon House. Beyond them the next of the Claydon villages — Steeple Claydon — is hidden in the skyline trees, but the steeple of its church can be seen amongst them. Steeples are rare in North Bucks, hence the village name.**

> **Claydon House has been the home of the Verney family from about 1543 to the present day. The west (nearest) end of the present house represents about one-third of a major rebuilding carried out in the eighteenth century (the rest of the rebuilt portion of the house was demolished in 1792 and replaced in the nineteenth century). The interior of the surviving eighteenth-century portion (which is now owned by the National Trust) is decorated in a sumptuous style scarcely rivalled in England.**

All Saints Church, standing on a mound beside the house, is the parish church of Middle Claydon and a reminder that, although Claydon House and church now stand in splendid isolation, the village once stretched out from its present site to join them.

Once through the kissing gate bear left to walk past the house and church following the terrace wall on the left. Follow the raised grassy causeway as it curves steadily left along the edge of the house's garden and then swings right and goes through a gate to join a drive from the house. Continue between the pair of lodge houses ahead, then turn right to set off along the road beyond.

After a third of a mile on the road turn left in front of Catherine Farm (immediately before a road comes in on the right) into the access road to Knowlhill Farm. The straightness of this ¾ mile-long road is emphasised by its two flanking rows of poplars. About 30 yards before reaching the first farm barn on the right, turn left on to the track which avoids the farm buildings and runs straight across a field into Romer Wood. Follow the track through the wood, and stay on it as it twists uphill across a fire break and on up through Greatsea Wood.

On emerging from the upper end of Greatsea Wood remain on the track as it runs along the left-hand side of two fields to the summit of the hill (seen between the lonely Finemerehill House on the right and a farm barn on the left).

As you cross these fields panoramic views westwards across the Vale of Aylesbury suddenly open up on the right. The large group of greenhouses on the low hill in the middle distance are part of Springhill Prison at Grendon Underwood.

On reaching the summit the track passes through a gate out of the field and forks. Take the left fork and set off along a green lane running along the summit, shortly to pass on the left-hand side of the barn. 100 yards beyond the barn the green lane ends, whereupon go through the gate directly ahead and follow the right-hand hedge along the margin of the field beyond. 60 yards before the corner of the field go through the gate on the right and then resume the course you have just been following, but now with the hedge on your left. (For the next 1¼ miles the route is beside this same hedge as it runs along the top of the hill, then down into the valley beyond, but it changes from side to side of the hedge twice more.)

Away on the right the tree-clad Waddesdon Hill is visible across the Vale with the Chiltern Hills forming the distant skyline.

Walk beside the hedgerow through this and the following field. In the second field two small ponds are passed; the first, surrounded by a fence, is well to your right, but the second, which is ringed by trees, is close to the hedgerow. 45 yards after the second pond (100 yards before reaching the corner of the field) go through the gate on the left to continue with the same hedge now on the right. In the corner of this field go through the gate on the right. Then bear left to maintain your course along the side of two further fields, with the hedge on your left once again, to join the Quainton to Botolph Claydon road at the bottom of the valley ahead.

As you descend towards the road, note the bare hill seen ahead to right on the other side of the valley (Grange Hill). Just below its summit you may detect the feint outline of a defensive ditch and bank which once ringed the hilltop (most easily visible in silhouette at each end of the hill). Prehistoric defended sites such as this are rare in this area.

On reaching the road turn left and follow it for a third of a mile; then turn right at the road junction by Hogshaw Farm (signposted to North Marston). The road you are now on passes a pair of semi-detached houses on the right, then crosses the route of the former Aylesbury–Verney Junction railway (cutting filled in on right, still visible on left). After this it passes a small farm (Hill End) on the left. Two hundred and fifty yards beyond Hill End Farm (and about 30 yards before a gate across the road), turn left through a gate into a field. Cross this field, aiming very slightly right to go beneath the overhead electricity line beside the midfield pole. Continue downhill to the bottom right-hand corner of the field and go through the hedge* ahead into the field beyond.

Once through the hedge the buildings of Middle Farm can be seen several fields away, ahead on the right; this and the following three fields are to be crossed on a straight course which passes close to the right-hand end of the farm buildings. Cross the field you have just entered heading diagonally to the right, at between 1 and 2 o'clock, to go through the gate in the middle of the far hedge (it is not visible until reached because it is set in an S-bend in an otherwise straight hedge line). Cross the ensuing field diagonally to the right, passing 5 yards to right of the midfield electricity line pole, to leave this field in the far right-hand corner.

Cross the footbridge and piece of fencing set in the hedge immediately to the right of the corner (ignoring a gate on your left leading into Middle Farm) and continue in the same diagonal direction across the following field to cross the far hedge* at a point directly opposite the barns of Middle Farm. In the next field cross diagonally to the left to go through the left-hand hedge* at its mid point into the second (furthest) of two fields visible behind it. Continue across the ensuing field diagonally to the right, aiming at the summit of the

*Stile needed and installation requested in 1988.

84

hill on which the village of Granborough is silhouetted. (If poor visibility hides Granborough stop *before* leaving the hedge, identify the second pylon from right, and then head slightly to left of it.) On reaching the field corner cross the footbridge spanning a drainage ditch, follow the fenced path beyond for 14 yards, then climb the stile in the right-hand hedge. Cross a smaller footbridge, turn left and go out of the field through a gate to reach the Granborough–Botolph Claydon road.

Turn left to walk along the road for a little over ¼ mile and leave it by turning right through the field gate opposite the entrance to Lower Farm. Now head diagonally to the left across this long triangular field to its far apex located between the second and third pylons to the north of the road you have just left. (The overhead electricity line running down the middle of this field is heading for the same place.)

As you walk this field, two of the Claydon villages are silhouetted on the ridge to your left. The left-hand line of houses is in Botolph Claydon. To the right of it the tower of East Claydon church marks the village from which you started.

Once in the apex go through the gate in the left-hand hedge and then forward beside the right-hand hedge of the following field and pass beneath the pylon line.

The pylon line follows the former course of the Aylesbury to Verney Junction railway, all trace of which has now vanished in this field. On your right, however, a low embankment survives to mark the site of the line in the next field. See page 21 for the history of this line.

Continue through the gate in the corner ahead and on beside the right-hand hedge in the next field to leave it through the gate projecting from the hedge across your route. Once in the following field maintain the same course, with the hedge now on the left as you climb gently into East Claydon. Shortly before the village is reached, join the metalled track which comes in above you on right from Sion Hill Farm and follow it through a gate and back into the village.

The Thame Valley

Walk 15	16¼ miles
O.S. 1:25,000 scale maps SP60, 70, 71	
(Pathfinder Series 1093, 1117)	

WHEATLEY — WATERPERRY — WATERSTOCK — SHABBINGTON —
THAME — CHEARSLEY — LOWER WINCHENDON — HARTWELL

Starting point: London Road, Wheatley, immediately west of Wheatley Bridge
(Grid ref: 611052)

A group of streams rising to the north and east of Aylesbury
have combined by the time they reach the town to form the
River Thame. From there the Thame flows generally south-
westwards in a broad valley which, particularly between the
towns of Aylesbury and Thame, is a haven of tranquillity. In
the past side streams have been dug to power water mills or to
improve river flow, so that today many sections of the valley
have two small rivers flowing one field apart. After prolonged
rain in winter the Thame floods spectacularly, inundating a
ribbon of valley bottom fields (and sections of this walk).

This walk goes upstream and follows the course of the river as
closely as possible. It splits naturally into two sections, one on
either side of the town of Thame.

Travel

*This is a straight walk which parallels the A418 road along which the Oxford
Bus Co.'s services 2 and 280 (Aylesbury–Thame–Wheatley–Oxford) provide
an hourly service every day except Sunday, when there is a 2-hourly service in
the afternoon only. Travel by bus to the start of the walk and alight at Wheatley
Bridge (at the eastern end of Wheatley village, near the Harvester Restaurant,
formerly the Bridge Hotel). For those walking only to or from Thame, please
see travel details on page 94.*

Refreshments

*None in Waterstock and Nether Winchendon. General store and pub in
Shabbington and Chearsley. Full range in Thame. Supermarket near the start
at Wheatley, and tea room at Waterperry House.*

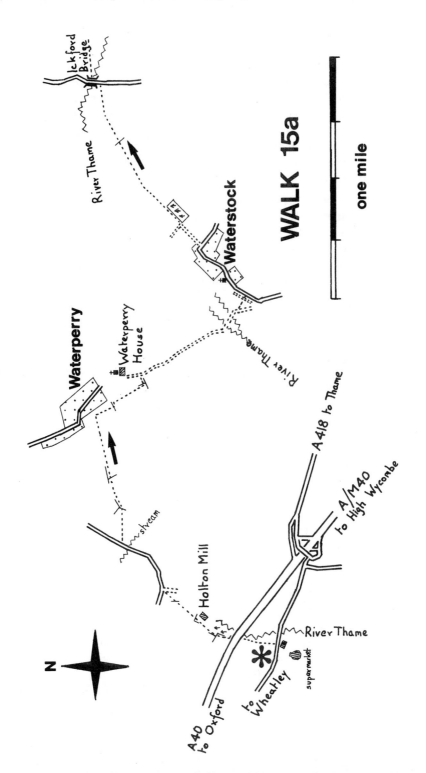

WALK 15a

one mile

Ickford Bridge

River Thame

Waterstock

Waterperry

Waterperry House

River Thame

A 418 to Thame

A/M40 to High Wycombe

stream

Holton Mill

River Thame

A40 to Oxford

to Wheatley

supermarket

N

Route

At Wheatley Bridge you are on one of the really old highways of England — the route from London to Gloucester and Hereford. A ford through the River Thame was recorded here in 956, a wooden bridge followed it, and this was probably rebuilt in stone in the thirteenth century. Further rebuildings followed, culminating in one in the early nineteenth century. The oldest identified part of the present bridge is the 500 year-old arch embedded in the eastern end.

Start in London Road at the Harvester Restaurant (between Wheatley Bridge and the petrol filling station). On the opposite side of the road to the restaurant descend the steps to a footbridge over a roadside stream and cross the stile into a meadow. Go straight ahead across the meadow to join the bank of the River Thame, then follow the river to go under the bridge which carries the Wheatley bypass, with its incessant roar of traffic.

Just before going beneath the bypass stop and look back for a view of the old Wheatley Bridge (best when there are no leaves on the trees).

On emerging from the concrete tunnel beneath the A40 bear left through a gateway into a field, then promptly turn right to walk away from the A40 along the right-hand side of the field.

The rather out-of-place tower block on the left-hand skyline is the Lady Spencer Churchill building, an outpost of Oxford Polytechnic.

In the next corner cross the footbridge and stile into the paddock ahead and maintain your course along the side of several small paddocks, following the fence on left. (This course takes you between the fence and the outbuildings of Holton Mill.) On climbing the stile out of the corner of the last paddock head at 1 o'clock across the field and the following small paddock to reach the left-hand end of the row of poplars. Once there, go over the stile beside the gate in the corner to come out on to the drive to Holton Mill. Turn left on it, then immediately right to set off along the Wheatley–Worminghall road. (Beware of speeding cars on this narrow, winding road.)

After ¼ mile on the road you cross a stone bridge over a stream. 50 yards beyond the bridge go over the stile* into the field on right and cross the field diagonally (aiming between 11 and 12 o'clock) to the far left-hand corner. In the corner cross the stile and "footbridge" in front of you and turn left along the left-hand side of the following field.

In the next corner cross the footbridge and stile ahead and, after emerging

*The M40 route, approved 1989, may cross near here — watch for path diversion.

from a small clump of field corner trees, continue ahead across the following field, diverging from the hedge on left and aiming for the cluster of houses immediately to left of the farm barns. On reaching the overhead electricity line which crosses your route (a few yards short of the back garden fences of the houses), turn right, follow the electricity wires and go through the gate in the field corner beside the barns. Beyond the gate take a few paces to left, then resume your course, now on a broad grass strip between an orchard and the grounds of Waterperry House. For the next mile you are following the route of the Oxfordshire Way long-distance footpath, which runs from Bourton-on-the-Water in the Cotswolds, to Henley-on-Thames.

On your left stands Waterperry House, built in the seventeenth and eighteenth centuries. Beside it, the parish church is a historic gem, with traces of Saxon work visible inside and with most of the building dating from before the fifteenth century. The house and its beautiful grounds now form the Waterperry Horticultural Centre. Its tea shop (the wooden hut to the left of the house, with access from the footpath via gateway almost opposite front of house) is open to the public daily except in January — it is well worth a visit.

When the grass strip ends at a fence and gate across your path turn left through an adjoining gate on to a fenced footpath which leads you along the side of the grounds to join an unmetalled track from Waterperry House. Turn right along the track and follow it for ½ mile, past an isolated thatched cottage to reach the picturesque house which was once Waterstock Mill.

Between the thatched cottage and the mill the track crosses the brick-built Bow Bridge over the stream which was formerly the by-pass stream for the watermill. The mill itself is the second of the River Thame's former watermills that you have passed (Holton Mill was the first); you will pass by or near another five sites on this walk.

Follow the track through gates into and out of the watermill's gardens. 20 yards beyond the second gate (opposite the triple garage) leave the drive via a pedestrian gate on left, climb the stile beyond, and cross the ensuing paddock, walking between horse jumps to climb the stile (without footstep) in the fence ahead. Cross an access drive, and go through the kissing gate in the thick hedge beyond, to emerge on the village road in Waterstock. Turn left along the road to walk into the centre of this delightful small village.

The present Waterstock House (on left) is the former service wing of a larger house built in 1787 and demolished in 1956. It is now a very smart horse training establishment.

WALK 15b

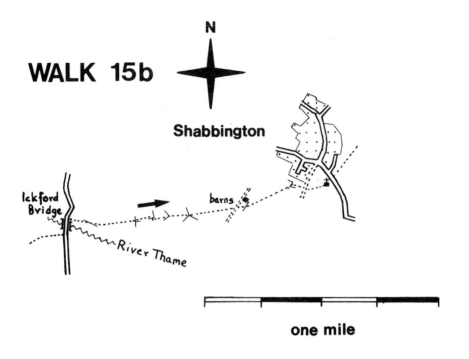

one mile

Near the centre of the village the road swings sharply to the right. Just beyond this corner, beside the war memorial, turn left along a farm access track to follow it out of the village until it turns sharp left in front of a gate across your path. Here leave the track, go through the gate, and maintain your course along a field edge, skirting a copse on your right.

At the end of the copse continue the same course out into the field ahead (usually this course is a junction between two crops) until you reach the mid-field crest of the shallow ridge ahead (usually another junction of crops). Then bear slightly right downhill, aiming across the field at 1 o'clock with a group of grey farm buildings visible far ahead, a little to left of your course. As you approach the hedge across the bottom of the field, aim for the tree located second to left of the lone barn in the hedgerow. Cross the horse jump placed in the hedge immediately to the left of this tree and, now on the level flood meadows of the Thame, bear diagonally right at 1 o'clock to pass close to the projecting corner of the hedge jutting into the field on your right (the right-hand of the two stone bridges at Ickford can be seen behind the corner). On passing this corner continue the same course to join the Tiddington–Ickford road via a stile and footbridge 30 yards to the right of the nearest of the Ickford Bridges. Turn left along the road.

The causewayed road you are now on once had considerable

importance as part of the direct route from the London–Oxford road (now the A40) at Milton Common to the mediaeval royal palace at Brill, and royal forest of Bernwood. The place at which it crossed the River Thame thus became one of the earliest road bridges in Buckinghamshire. There was certainly a bridge in existence here by 1237, although the present one is probably a sixteenth-century replacement of the earlier structure. (Note that the historic bridge is the first of the two which you reach — it has a county boundary mark dated 1685 on it; the other bridge is a later structure to let floodwaters through the causeway.)

Between the two bridges climb the stile on right. Cross the bridge over the ditch in front of you, then bear slightly left to go through the broad gap in the left-hand hedge 100 yards ahead. Maintain the same course across the following field, passing close to left of the midfield clump of hawthorns. This course brings you to cross the stile situated in the hedge/fence ahead, about 70 yards to right of the far left-hand corner. Beyond the stile cross the almost unnecessary footbridge, continue ahead beside the hedge on your right, and in the corner ahead, turn right to cross a footbridge.

From the far end of the footbridge bear half left to follow a nearly straight course across three fields to reach the right-hand corner of a pair of barns seen ⅓ mile ahead. Leave the first field over a stile in the left-hand corner, continue across the second to go through the left-hand of two field gates in the hedge ahead, and on across the third to reach the right-hand corner of the barns. (A farm track is crossed shortly before the barns are reached.)

Cross the footbridge in the hedge just to the right of the barns. Now with Shabbington village close ahead, go diagonally left across the next field, aiming just left of the squat tower of the church, to reach the stile situated 15 yards to the right of the far left-hand corner. Once over the stile walk up the right-hand side of a paddock and skirt round the left side of the bungalow ahead. Cross the farm track at the top of the field (stiles on each side are not quite opposite each other) and bear left across the next field to a stile leading into the churchyard. Skirt the church tower to reach the village road.

Shabbington, perched above the valley of the Thame, is typical of so many English villages in that, in spite of its long history, it has few claims to fame and only a scatter of older buildings to remind of its past. The pub is down the hill to the right; to reach the village shop go uphill to the crossroads, then bear right.

Cross the road, climb the stile directly opposite the churchyard gate, and walk across the hillside so that you gradually diverge from the row of

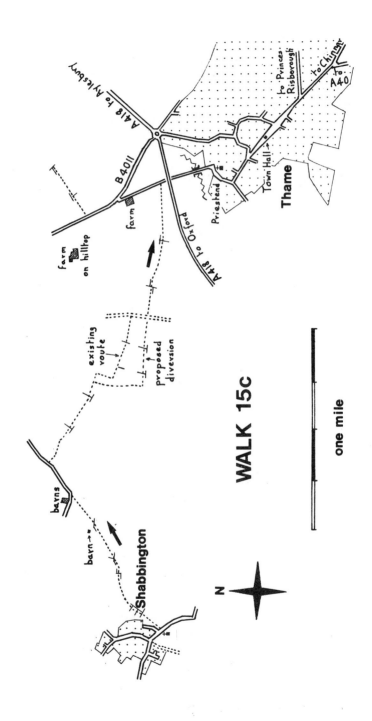

WALK 15c

one mile

N

bungalows on your left. Go over the stile and footbridge in the middle of the fence/hedge ahead. Continue along the right-hand (lower) side of two small paddocks, leaving each by a stile in the corner ahead. On again for ¼ mile beside the curving right-hand hedge along the lower edge of the next field (ignore a small embayment to the right early on). Go through the first gate in the right-hand hedge after the embayment (the gate projects into the field across your route) and maintain the same course, now beside the hedge on your left.

At the point (60 yards beyond the gate) where the left-hand curve of the hedge changes to a right-hand curve, turn left over a footbridge/stile* into the corner of another field.

Maintain the course followed in the previous field to cross this one diagonally to join and follow the left-hand hedge as you go beneath the first of two overhead electricity lines. Go over the stile on your left 40 yards beyond the second electricity line. Now, leaving a nearby barn on your left, bear right at between 1 and 2 o'clock to walk along the middle of this irregularly shaped field. On this course you diverge from the overhead electricity line on your left and come out on to the Shabbington–Long Crendon road through a gate in the furthest corner of the field (seen just to the right of some ramshackle barns visible over the hedge).

In this field you are walking obliquely over "ridge and furrow" — the fossilized remains of a mediaeval open field cultivation system in which a farmer would hold unfenced strips (represented by the ridges) scattered in ones and twos all over the parish. The "ridge and furrow" effect was obtained by each farmer ploughing soil up on to his strip, away from the furrow which marked the strip's boundary.

Turn right along the road for 350 yards, then leave it via the stile beside the second gate on right. (The gate is on the outside of a left-hand bend in the road.) With the road squarely behind you set off, gently uphill at first, beside the right-hand hedge of this and the following field, crossing the stiles and footbridge in the hedge between them. Cross the footbridge and stile in the far right-hand corner of the second of these fields, and continue beside the right-hand hedge in the next until the hedge turns sharp right.

Pause at this corner on the edge of a large field which is usually subdivided into numerous pig pens. At the time of writing (October 1988) the course of the next ½ mile of this path was subject to a formal application for diversion.

Until the diversion is approved **your route is to leave the hedge corner and go ahead for a few paces between electric fences, then to turn right along a service track between electric fences. This course takes you past the end of a**

*Footbridge damaged; replacement requested in 1988.

midfield hedge, then straight on to go through a gap in the hedge ahead (at which the electric fences end) and straight on again across the following field to the stile in the fence ahead. This stile flanks a farm track; turn right along it for 120 yards to the field corner. Then turn left to climb the horse jump in the fence and set off at a right angle to the track, walking along the edge of a field beside the fence on right.

When (and if) the diversion is approved* stay with the hedge as it turns right at the corner and walk beside it down the side of the field. On reaching the next corner of this field turn left and follow the straight boundary on your right along the edge of this and the three following fields; you will cross a farm track between the last two of these fields.

Once the farm track is behind you, so too is the diversion proposal. Cross the stile/footbridge in the corner ahead and maintain the same course, now beside the left-hand hedge, through the next two fields, as the Thame bypass gets closer. At the far left-hand corner of the second field climb the stile to come out on to the carriageway of the former Thame–Bicester road.

This section of B class road was abandoned in 1980 when it was cut by the new Thame bypass and replaced by the new alignment which can be seen converging on it above Thame Mead Farm. It remains a pedestrian right of way, giving an impressive entrance to Thame over the multiple-arched Thame Bridge and in past the Prebendal and parish church.

If ending your walk here, turn right, cross the bypass, and follow the old road into Thame. About 150 yards after passing the parish church turn left at the road junction and follow High Street to the Town Hall, where all buses stop.

If continuing the walk turn left and walk up the old road to join the Thame–Long Crendon road and go forward along it. Then continue route description below.

Thame Point for leaving or joining the walk	9¼ miles on to Hartwell O.S. 1:25,000 scale maps SP70, 71 (Pathfinder Series 1093, 1117)

Travel

Motorists can park in the broad, quiet road called Priestend beside the parish church (grid ref: 703063).

*If the diversion is approved, waymarks at this point should indicate the change of route.

Bus travellers have the joint Aylesbury Bus/Oxford Bus services 2, 260, 280 (Aylesbury–Thame–Oxford) which, on weekdays, provide a half-hourly service between Aylesbury and Thame and an hourly one on to Oxford. On Sundays there is a 2-hourly interval service from Aylesbury to Oxford in the afternoon and evening only by Oxford Bus.

On weekdays Bee Line and Oxford Bus services 232, 331 and 332 run roughly every two hours from High Wycombe via Chinnor to Thame. You can return from Aylesbury to High Wycombe on Bee Line services 323 and 324 (half-hourly on weekdays, 2-hourly on Sundays) or by train (roughly 2-hourly on weekdays only).

Refreshments

See notes at the beginning of this walk.

Route

Alight from all buses at Thame Town Hall and, leaving the front entrance of the Town Hall behind you, walk to the north-west (parish church) end of the High Street, where the road ends at a "T" junction. Turn right into Priestend and follow the road past the church and over Thame Bridge. (The gate across the road just beyond the church marks the point where, since 1980, this former B class road has been downgraded to a more-than-adequate footpath.)

Cross the Thame by-pass and continue ahead uphill to join the Thame–Long Crendon road and go forward along it. The pavement changes sides in front of the walled farmhouse. 140 yards further on cross the stile between the pair of gates on the right and set off downhill beside the fence/hedge on your left through two fields. Go through the gate in the bottom left-hand corner of the second field and bear left at 11 o'clock over a third field to cross the stile/footbridge in the hedge ahead (in front of the nearest building on the industrial site beyond). Once in the factory complex take a few paces to right, then quickly bear left to follow a roadway right across the site, between the main buildings on your left, and a stockyard on right. Half way through the site go through the pedestrian gates in the fences flanking another roadway which divides up the complex. (The legal route through this site is a straight line, but you may find it temporarily obstructed by parked lorries or stored products.)

In 1937 a resident of Thame began to dig for gravel in low-lying fields here beside the River Thame. He washed, graded and sold the gravel on the site. Gradually he turned to the manufacture of concrete roof tiles and then to small concrete products, mostly for farms. From this small beginning grew Crendon Concrete, a firm with a national reputation whose

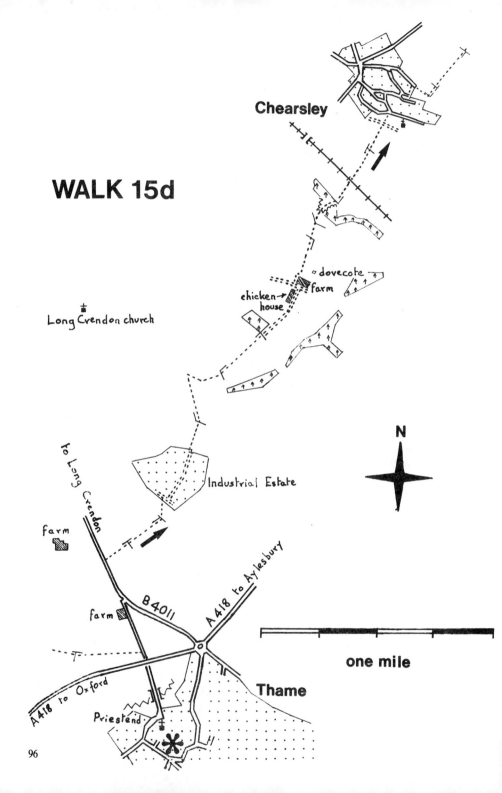

Chearsley

WALK 15d

dovecote

chicken→ farm
house

Long Crendon church

Industrial Estate

N

to Long Crendon

farm

farm

B 4011

A 418 to Aylesbury

one mile

A 418 to Oxford

Thame

Priestend

products you can see around you. As the years passed, other firms came to the site and today you see a 50-acre industrial estate, sited somewhat incongruously in open countryside where one man once dug for gravel.

At the far end of the site return to the fields via a stile beside an overhead electricity line pole and go straight ahead beside the hedge on right.

The water seen through the hedge on right is in the gravel pits from which Crendon Concrete developed. Today all raw materials are brought in from other sites.

Climb the stile beside the gate in the fence/hedge ahead and follow the left-hand margin of the ensuing field to its next corner. (The tower of Long Crendon church becomes prominent on the skyline on your left.) At the corner stay in the field, turn right and continue, now beside another hedge on left.

In the next corner cross the footbridge and stile and continue ahead uphill along the left-hand side of the field towards the wood on the skyline. In the top left-hand corner go through the gate ahead and maintain your course, now on a fenced track and initially with the wood on your left.

As you approach the summit in winter you can see the roofs of Notley Abbey amongst trees in the valley ahead on your right. More about the Abbey can be found on page 55.

Your route crosses the track leading down to the Abbey in the middle of a farm complex beside a modern stone-built farmhouse. At the crossing bear left across the other track towards the nearest electricity line pole, climb the stile behind it (invisible until reached) then bear right to skirt behind the silos and the farm barn. At the end of the barn go to the nearest electricity line pole, then bear left to walk over the summit and downhill beside the scrubby remains of a hedge on your right (see page 54 for details of the massive stone dovecote on right).

Cross the stile in the bottom corner and continue beside the sinuous right-hand fence as it skirts the overgrown remains of Notley Abbey's mediaeval fishponds on right. Climb the stile attached to a willow in the right-hand fence 30 yards before the bottom corner of the field. Now on the level, maintain almost the same course across a narrow meadow to a stile and footbridge over a tributary of the River Thame. From the far side of the bridge continue ahead on a winding path through a plantation. (You are walking parallel to the stream a few yards on right, but lush summer vegetation tends to hide it.) At the other side of the plantation ignore the gate on right and, instead, go through the gateway in the fence ahead and uphill along the right-hand side of a sloping field to reach the railway.

Cross the Marylebone–Banbury railway by stiles and staircases, and maintain your course beside the fence along the upper margin of two fields with Chearsley church tower becoming visible slightly to right ahead, and the broad valley of the River Thame to your right. At the end of the second field climb the stile beside the gate in the corner, cross the farm track and stile beyond it, then with the houses of Chearsley ahead maintain the same course across the next field to cross a stile found just to right of the electricity line pole.

For notes on Chearsley see page 53

Cross Church Lane and go ahead up Shupps Lane (opposite). Turn first right into Watts Green, and first right again to go down Dark Lane. At the bottom of the lane (at Elm Brook Close) bear left, then immediately right down a short lane which ends at a gate and stile. Cross the stile into a field, turn sharp left to walk beside a garden fence, and cross the stile in the corner ahead. Traverse a short neck of garden, climb the stile opposite and continue on a hedged path to emerge on a village street. Turn right along the street for a few yards to its end, then climb the stile beside the gate and continue down the left-hand side of the field.

At the point where the fence goes away to the left, turn left through the gate and set off along the right-hand margin of two fields. At the end of the second one cross the footbridge and stile in the corner ahead. Now maintain almost the same direction over the large ensuing field, heading for the solitary electricity line pole in the far right-hand corner.

On your right, on the far side of the River Thame, are the buildings of Cuddington Mill, another of the former water-mills in this valley.

As you approach the above electricity line pole you see that it stands beside cattle pens and a field gate. Go through the cattle pen gates on to the road, turn right, then immediately left at the road junction and walk along the road to Ashendon. After 150 yards turn right over the stile in the hedge, then bear slightly left across the field to the projecting corner of the hedge ahead. On reaching that corner, continue the same course but now with a ditch on right beside you. 100 yards before reaching the corner ahead (at the point where a hedge comes in on right in the adjoining field) bear left across your field to the far left corner. There cross a stile on to the village road in Nether Winchendon opposite a timber-framed farmhouse. Turn right along the road to reach the church.

Nether Winchendon is one of those villages which never loses its magic. Small and very peaceful, with a harmonious group of buildings from several centuries, it is a classic English

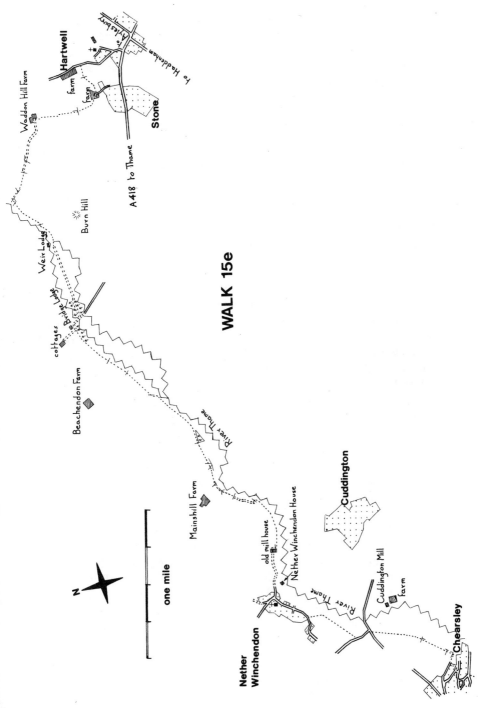

WALK 15e

N

one mile

Hartwell

farm

to Aylesbury

to Haddenham

Stone

A418 to Thame

Wadden Hill Farm

Weir Lodge

Burn Hill

Bridge Lodge

cottages

Beachendon Farm

Mainshill Farm

River Thame

old mill house

Nether Winchendon House

Cuddington

Cuddington Mill

farm

River Thame

Nether Winchendon

Chearsley

99

village. It is also an example of the changing character of so many villages in the twentieth century, as their agricultural workforce has diminished. The village pub closed in 1919, the one village shop ceased to trade in the 1960's, and the school was converted into a private house in 1975. An hourly bus service was replaced by two buses per day in 1970.

Please turn to page 9 for notes on Nether Winchendon House.

At the church take the right fork and follow the narrow winding road past the entrance to Nether Winchendon House and on until it ends in front of the buildings of the village's former watermill (now a private house). On reaching the mill go ahead on the track *between* the barns to the left of the mill house; at the end of the last barn turn right, climb the stile beside the gate, and follow a short track behind the barn to enter a meadow beside the River Thame.

Turn left on the meadow and walk beside the left-hand hedge with the mill behind you and the Thame winding 100 yards away on the right. (The village of Cuddington is on the hill on right.) 30 yards before the meadow ends as the Thame closes in, turn left through the gate and then quickly resume your course, but now on a fenced farm track along the lower side of a field. When the track ends, continue straight ahead across the lower end of the field, to climb the stile in the hedge ahead.

With Mainshill Farm now standing above on left, bear right to walk along the bottom side of the field, and go over a stile and footbridge in the corner ahead. Continue beside the ditch along the bottom of the next field, go through the gate in the corner ahead, bear slightly left across the narrow neck of a field, and through the gate in the hedge opposite.

On again across the next field, with the ditch 20–40 yards away on right, to go over the pair of stiles visible ahead 40 yards from the right-hand corner of the field. Skirt along the edge of the ensuing copse on your right and stop to get your bearings when you get to the end of it. The field boundary turns away to the right, but your route goes ahead to meet the river at the left-hand one of the three low bushy trees seen 200 yards ahead.

Having joined the river, continue ahead along its bank. (Beachendon Farm, the next of the skyline farms, becomes visible ahead on the left.) On reaching the field corner, turn left to follow the hedge for 60 yards, then turn right to climb the stile in it. Now bear left, aiming at between 10 and 11 o'clock across the next field to cross a stile in the hedge ahead 50 yards from the right-hand corner of the field.

On your way across this field you come alongside one arm of a mediaeval moated site. Although the moat is now dry and its "island" deserted, this is a fine example of the loneliness of many such sites. For more about moated sites see page 127.

Once over the stile go straight ahead across the lower end of the next field (50 yards out from the river) to cross a footbridge in the hedge ahead. On ahead again across a final field to the outermost point of the clump of trees which projects into the field 300 yards ahead. Continue along the edge of the trees to go out through a gate on to an estate road in front of Bridge Lodge.

You are now in the Eythrope Estate which is one of the areas of parkland surrounding the seven great houses built in the Vale of Aylesbury by members of the Rothschild family in the second half of the last century. The house at the centre of Eythrope Estate is The Pavilion, built in 1883 for Alice de Rothschild.

Maintain your course on the road past Bridge Lodge and round to the right over Eythrope Bridge.

The waterfall beside the bridge is on the site of a watermill which probably went out of use in the seventeenth century. In the 1880's the mill site was dammed so as to raise the level of the millstream to form an ornamental lake along the south side of Eythrope Park. In The Pavilion's heyday Rothschild guests were conveyed by launch to a lakeside lodge for afternoon tea in summer.

60 yards beyond Eythrope Bridge (half way between it and the bridge over the River Thame) turn left on to an access track. Follow this for half a mile, first through a wood, then along a causeway across a meadow.

Towards the end of the woodland section (when the track becomes concreted) look left for glimpses across the lake and park to Eythrope Pavilion, partly hidden amongst trees.

Once on the causeway you will see a prominent small round hill across the valley on your right. This is Burn Hill which, in spite of its artificial appearance, is actually a natural feature. To confuse matters, its top has been used as a prehistoric burial site.

Just before reaching the stables at the end of the causeway take to the fenced path on right to pass alongside the stables and cross a footbridge.

Beneath the bridge water roars over a weir into the original course of the River Thame, leaving the artificial cut heading for Eythrope Lake and waterfall. Facing the bridge across the water is Weir Lodge, one of the attractive properties in

Eythrope Park. Note the "five arrows" insignia (the crest of the Rothschilds) on its gable end.

Continue ahead beside the river on a narrow meadow which widens out at its end to enclose a small clump of trees. Ignoring stiles to left and right of the trees, bear slightly left through the clump and go through a field gate (hidden until reached) in a corner in the hedge/fence in front of you. Bear left beyond the gate to follow the fence/hedge on left along the bottom side of the field. When a gate projects into your path go through it to rejoin the river and continue ahead beside it in a fenced grass strip.

Now, with the modern industries of Aylesbury suddenly dominating the view ahead, go through the gate in front of you and turn right to leave the River Thame for the last time. Walk up the right-hand side of the field, go through the gate in the corner ahead, and continue beside the right-hand hedge in the following field. When the hedge turns away to right, leave it and continue ahead downhill across the remainder of the field. Join the farm track at the next hedge and walk it across the following field to go through the gap in the corner of the hedge at the top. Continue in the same direction beside the winding hedge on your left along the side of a sloping field to reach the buildings of Whaddon Hill Farm.

The "North Bucks Way" waymarks which you have been following since Eythrope Bridge indicate the local long-distance footpath running from the Ridgeway Path in the Chiltern Hills above Great Kimble, to the new city of Milton Keynes. The route was inaugurated in 1972.

On reaching the farm, turn right in front of the barns and after passing the last barn bear slightly left to go into the upper corner of the field beyond it. Continue beside the hedge down the right-hand side of the field. When the hedge on right ends, move a few yards to the left to continue down the side of the following field, now with the hedge on left. In the bottom corner of this field go over the footbridge and stile *ahead* and continue the same course uphill across the next field to reach the hedge opposite. Now turn left and walk beside the hedge to leave the field through two gates which take you into and out of Upper Hartwell Farm and on to the road beyond.

50 yards after coming on to the road, leave it over the stile on left before the thatched cottage. Go straight across the next field, to the telegraph pole on the far side (the route takes you in and out of grassy hollows marking the site of a disused quarry). Go through the gate at the end of the field (just beyond the pole) and across the middle of the final field to the gate on to a road.

Turn right and walk up the road. At the top of the short hill a walled footpath goes off on the left to run beside Hartwell's village graveyard.

Follow it, and emerge to continue along a grassy street in the attractive village of Hartwell.

The parish church whose roofless shell stands behind the wall on left was built in 1753–5 and is one of the most important churches of the Early Gothic Revival. It was sited so as to appear in views from nearby Hartwell House. The church's present condition results from a theft of lead from the roof in the 1940's, leading to rapid decay of the roof structure and its collapse in the 1960's.

The grassy street ends when it meets the access road to Hartwell House in front of the latter's stables. Turn right along the access road.

Hartwell House was built in the seventeenth century, and enlarged in the eighteenth. From 1809 to 1814 it was the residence of the French king in exile — Louis XVIII. The French court took up residence in the village of Hartwell so that, for five years, this quiet Buckinghamshire retreat buzzed with foreign tongues as the French nobility passed their exiled years. The international flavour returned when, from 1956 to 1983, Hartwell House was a private secretarial college for girls from all over the world. After this closed the house was extensively renovated in 1987–9 for a new role as a very exclusive hotel.

Bear left at the next "T" junction and follow the road over a hump bridge across a garden path linking two parts of Hartwell House's grounds. Suddenly you reach the Aylesbury–Oxford road (A418) and the end of the walk. Turn left for the bus stop for Aylesbury-bound services (this side of the road) or those for Thame, Wheatley and Oxford on the opposite side.

The Aylesbury Ring

Walk 16	31¼ miles
See individual sections for relevant O.S. maps	

WENDOVER — GREAT KIMBLE — DINTON — WADDESDON — HARDWICK — WEEDON — ROWSHAM — HULCOTT — PUTTENHAM — BUCKLAND — ASTON CLINTON — WENDOVER

Starting points are given at the beginning of each section of the Ring.

Our last walk is the brainchild of John Maples and Ray Knowles of the Ramblers' Association's Aylesbury Group. With their extensive local footpath knowledge they devised a route which is full of interest and which is capable of providing anything from a modest family ramble along one section to a challenge for the long-distance walker who wants to complete the whole 31¼ mile Ring in one day.

It is also a route which demonstrates just how successful our town planning authorities have been over the years in controlling the spread of development. The route of the Ring is never more than 5 miles from the centre of Aylesbury; sometimes the distance is as little as 3 miles. Nevertheless this route passes through countryside and villages which seem remote from modern development. From occasional vantage points on the Ring one looks down on the distant spread of Aylesbury with its homes for 50,000 people and its factories; the view only heightens one's awareness of the peaceful rural surroundings of the walk. At other times Aylesbury could be 50 miles away!

Travel

At seven points on its circuit the Ring cuts across main bus routes radiating from Aylesbury. Unless you are planning to walk the whole Ring in a day we suggest that you catch a bus out from Aylesbury to your selected starting point, and another one back to Aylesbury from your destination. There is ample public car parking space in Aylesbury within a short distance of its Bus Station. Details of public transport services from Aylesbury are given at the beginning of each section.

Wendover The start of the Ring	3½ miles on to Great Kimble O.S. 1:25,000 scale map SP80 (Pathfinder Series 1118) Our route map 16a

Travel

There is an hourly train service to Wendover every day on the Aylesbury–Amersham–Marylebone line.

Aylesbury Bus and Red Rover operate services 55 and 56 (Aylesbury–Wendover–Halton Camp) twice an hour on weekdays and hourly on Sundays. Red Rover route 28 (Aylesbury–Wendover–Tring) is less frequent and does not run on Sundays. Alight from all buses at Wendover Clock Tower.

There is a public car park beside Wendover Library, on the south side of High Street.

Refreshments on the first section

Pubs, cafes and shops in Wendover; there is a public toilet in the car park off the High Street. A pub and a general store at Butlers Cross, and a pub at Great Kimble.

Route

The centre of Wendover is a most attractive Conservation Area based on the High Street which slopes uphill from the Clock Tower. It was formerly a coaching town on the London–Aylesbury road. The broad market place above the war memorial (known as the Manor Waste) has a street market on Thursdays. Opposite it the antique shop with prominent vertical timber framing is one of the oldest buildings in Wendover, dating from the sixteenth century or earlier.

Start the walk at the Clock Tower and proceed up High Street and its continuation (Pound Street) beyond the mini-roundabout. After passing the last house on the left the road goes over the railway at Wendover Station and then beneath a pylon line. Leave the road by turning right down the track starting beside the first house beyond the pylon line. (Some time after 1991 the proposed Wendover bypass will cut through here, probably necessitating a path diversion at this point.)

When the track turns right to enter a playing field, continue straight ahead along the right-hand side of a large, sloping field. After 130 yards the hedge on right turns away. At this point strike out diagonally to left across the large field, aiming at 11 o'clock towards the right-hand one of a trio of distant

105

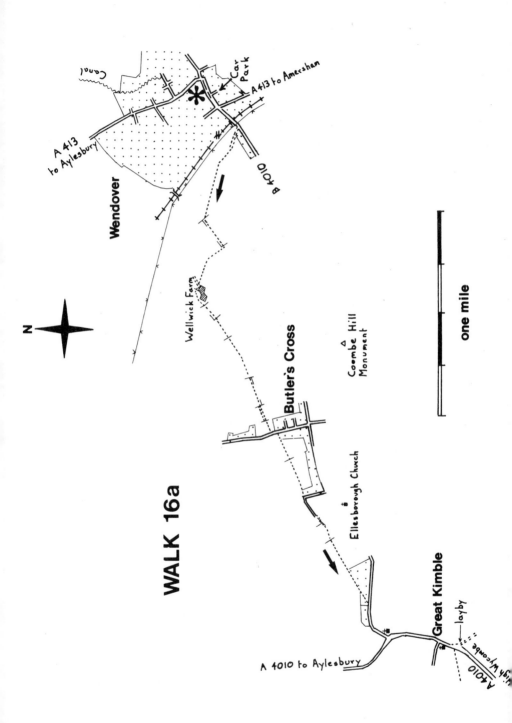

WALK 16a

Wendover

Canal

A 413 to Aylesbury

Car Park

A 413 to Amersham

B 4010

N

Wellwick Farm

Butler's Cross

Coombe Hill Monument

Ellesborough Church

Great Kimble

layby

A 4010 to Aylesbury

A 4010

High Wycombe

one mile

houses which are partially hidden by trees. Leave the field over the stile in the left-hand fence opposite the bridge over the railway, pass beneath the electricity cables, and continue beside the hedge on your right in the next field.

In this field a monument is visible almost in front of you on top of the Chiltern escarpment. It was erected in 1904 to commemorate those killed in the Boer War. It stands on Coombe Hill (852 ft), one of the highest points in the Chilterns.

Climb the stile in the field corner ahead, turn right, and follow the baulk running between two fields; this shortly turns diagonally left to head for the barns of Wellwick Farm. Cross the drive leading from the farm to the houses and pass down the right-hand side of the barns to climb a stile beside a pair of gates. Bear diagonally left across the ensuing field (aiming at 10 o'clock) to pass close along the back of Wellwick Farm house and climb the stile in the field corner (not visible until you are behind the house). This brings you into the orchard beside the farmhouse.

Wellwick Farm house (or Manor) dates from 1616 and looks very impressive with its massive octagonal chimneys. The front was rebuilt in Georgian times but, round at the back, some of the original building can still be seen (note the stone-mullioned window).

Proceed ahead along the right-hand side of the orchard and go over the stile in the corner ahead. For the next ¾ mile your route is almost a straight line to the hamlets of Chalkshire and Butlers Cross, beyond which the tower of Ellesborough church is visible intermittently ahead. Follow the right-hand side of the field beyond the orchard, cross the stile in the end corner, and continue straight across the middle of the following field. Climb the stile in front of you and on uphill across the next field to the stile beside the gate on the skyline.

Ahead is the silhouette of Ellesborough church tower and, to the left of it, the dramatic treeless outline of the chalk spur called Cymbeline's Castle. The "castle" name derives from the earthworks of an Iron Age fortress on the summit which are not visible from this angle. To your right the wide view over the Vale of Aylesbury is terminated by the line of hills through Quainton, Waddesdon, Ashendon and Brill.

Climb the stile in front of you and proceed, now gently downhill, beside a fence on your left towards the hamlet of Butlers Cross. At the bottom of the field continue ahead on a hedged track, then across a final field to reach the road.

You are in the parish of Ellesborough, which is unusual for the Vale of Aylesbury in that it has no central village. Instead it consists of a scatter of small hamlets, of which the one called Ellesborough (which includes the parish church) is not the largest. The two hamlets you are now approaching are Butlers Cross (the largest in the parish) on the left, and the attractively named Chalkshire on the right.

Turn left along the road for 50 yards, then right, over a stile, and along the fenced footpath which starts beside the bungalow. When the fenced section of path ends, climb the stile and continue straight ahead across the next field and into a short green lane beside a bungalow on the edge of the hamlet of Ellesborough. Join the village road on the outside of a corner and maintain your previous direction, now on the road, with the church tower visible on its hillock high on your left. After a few more yards, fine topiary on the right screens a real English country garden.

When the road ends (beside a thatched flint cottage) climb the stile in front of you (to the left of the gate) and maintain your direction beside the fence on the right. After some 50 yards go through the gate on your right, then resume the same direction in this and the next field (crossing a stile between them) but now with the fence on your left. At the far corner of the second field go through the gate and continue ahead across a third field to the outer corner of a row of gardens. Straight on beside the bottom of the gardens with dwellings on your left before continuing on a fenced path. At the end of the path turn left in a front garden to emerge on the B4010 (Upper Icknield Way).

Turn right to walk along the road for nearly 400 yards to its junction with the A4010 (Aylesbury–Princes Risborough) road.

The tiny All Saints church on your left at the road junction is old — most of it dates from the thirteenth century. It contains a remarkable series of fourteenth-century wall paintings which, regrettably, have suffered from decay down the centuries. The church is also notable in that Ellesborough church is only just over half a mile behind you and Great Kimble church is a quarter-mile ahead. This togetherness is a rather extreme result of the tendency for parishes along the foot of the Chiltern Hills to be long and narrow so as to include within their boundaries a portion of good clay farmland down in the Vale as well as a portion of woodland for grazing and timber supplies up on the hills. Such was the attraction of this type of location that villages were squeezed

in along the foot of the Chilterns. The most extreme example locally occurs at Horsenden, near Princes Risborough, where the parish is less than 300 yards wide in the vicinity of the church.

Turn left along the A4010 and continue, first uphill to the Bernard Arms Hotel, then downhill past Great Kimble parish church.

It was at this church that John Hampden made his protest against the payment of Ship Money (in 1635) which was a much publicised step in the chain of events which led to the start of the English Civil War. A document connected with the event hangs in the church.

Great Kimble Point for joining or leaving the Ring	6 miles on to Dinton Castle O.S. 1:25,000 scale maps SP70, 71, 80 (Pathfinder Series 1093, 1117, 1118) Our route maps 16b, 16c

Travel

Bee Line bus services 323, 324 (Aylesbury–Princes Risborough–High Wycombe) call at Great Kimble every half hour on weekdays and every two hours on Sundays. Aylesbury Bus/Bee Line joint service X15 (Reading–High Wycombe–Aylesbury–Milton Keynes) calls four times on weekdays and twice on Sundays. Alight at the Bernard Arms.

Cars can be parked in the lay-by off the A4010 just south of Great Kimble church.

Refreshments on the next section

Pubs at Great Kimble and Ford; no other facilities.

Route

In the dip in the road just beyond the church, opposite the start of a lay-by, turn right through a kissing gate into a field. (You have now joined the North Bucks Way, which runs from the Chilterns to Milton Keynes.) Cross this field diagonally towards the brick-built Old Grange farmhouse to reach the stile situated beside a telegraph pole (as you cross the field, this pole is seen in front of the farmhouse).

The complex layout of rectangular mounds which covers the far end of this field is possibly the site of a group of houses dating from the mediaeval period when Great Kimble

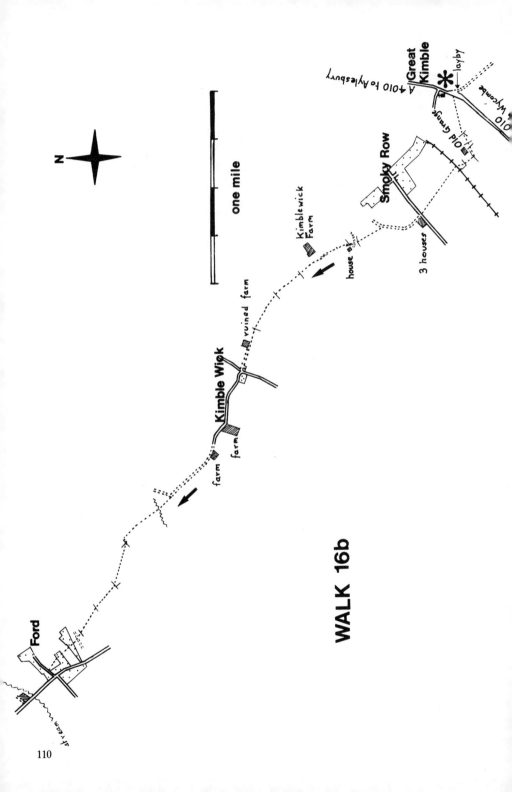

one mile

N

Great Kimble

A 4010 to Aylesbury

layby

4010 to Wycombe

Old Grange

Smoky Row

3 houses

house

Kimblewick Farm

ruined farm

Kimble Wick

farm

farm

Ford

WALK 16b

extended in this direction. First, however, you pass the arrow-head shape of earthworks which *appear* to be a defensive position thrown up during the Civil War.

Go over the stile into the field beside the Old Grange and cross it to climb the stile seen ahead in front of a small thatched summerhouse. Cross the drive leading to the farmhouse and the stile opposite, then go diagonally to the right across the corner of the next field to climb the stile visible immediately to the right of a field gate (50 yards to left of the fine timber-clad barn). Change direction to continue along the right-hand side of the following field (beside one arm of the moat which once surrounded the Old Grange) and in the next corner climb the stile into the right-hand of two fields ahead. Bear very slightly right in this field to cross the Aylesbury–Princes Risborough branch railway (farm gate on each side of crossing).

Once across the railway you are confronted by a large, generally featureless field. The main group of houses in Smoky Row is away on the right of the field and a detached group of four dwellings is visible almost straight ahead. Your course is straight across the field to the thatched cottage at the right-hand end of this detached group (in 1988 a surviving isolated midfield tree stood about 20 yards to the right of this course).

On reaching the far side of the field go out through the gate, cross the B4009 (Lower Icknield Way) and continue directly opposite along the hedged bridleway which starts beside the thatched cottage. After nearly ¼ mile on the bridleway, just before drawing level with the lone farmhouse (only its roof and chimney-stacks are visible from the lane) seen across the field on the left, you reach a pair of gates facing each other on either side of the bridleway. Go through the left-hand gate and diagonally to right across the field, aiming just to right of the low shed on the right-hand side of the house. Pass through the gate located at the point where the field boundary ahead changes from a hedge to a fence.

With the southern part of the Vale of Aylesbury spread out in front of you, continue ahead, going across the drive to the house and downhill following the hedge/fence on your left in two fields. Immediately before drawing level with the first of the buildings of Kimblewick Farm on your right, leave this field over the stile beside the *second* gate on left, then turn right to resume your direction of travel, but now with the curving fence/hedge on your right. Continue in the same general direction along the right-hand side of this and the three following fields, using a stile, a footbridge and then a gate in the respective field corners. Half way along the side of the last of these fields, when passing the partially ruined buildings of Manor Farm, go through the gate projecting across your path and maintain the same direction along a fenced farm track.

You are approaching the hamlet of Kimble Wick, which is best known as the location of the kennels for the Vale of Aylesbury Hunt. Some 40 pairs of foxhounds are kept here, together with horses for the huntsman and whipper-in. Their day starts early so you are unlikely to meet the pack on their exercise runs.

On entering the hamlet cross straight over the road and continue along the minor road opposite. This winds past several isolated cottages and farm buildings, becomes an unmetalled green lane, and then bends *sharp* right ¾ mile after its beginning (just before two parallel overhead electricity lines cross the lane). At the latter bend maintain your course by leaving the lane through the gate which is almost in front of you. Cross the field (aiming at 1 o'clock) to the stile and footbridge in the hedge ahead and, once over them, continue in the same direction up the right-hand side of the field beyond. On reaching the top corner stay in this field and turn left for 40 yards, then turn right and go through the gate in the hedge.

The hamlet of Ford is now just visible in the trees ahead. Bear diagonally left across the middle of the next field, aiming at the left-hand end of the houses in Ford. Cross the stile and footbridge just to the right of the field corner and, with the hedge squarely behind you, go straight across the ensuing field to pass through the left-hand one of the two gaps in the hedge in front of you. Aim slightly to the left (between 11 and 12 o'clock) across the next field, to leave it over a stile in the fence ahead, seen just to the left of the thatched cottage (the nearest house in Ford).

Cross the drive to the cottage, climb the stile in the hedge ahead and continue across two paddocks (with a stile between) to a fourth stile seen to the left of a white-walled house. Maintain the same course through two front gardens and over three more stiles before heading at between 11 and 12 o'clock across a small paddock to emerge via a stile on a village road just to the right of the Dinton Hermit public house.

The name of the Dinton Hermit pub commemorates John Biggs, a secretary of Simon Mayne of Dinton Hall (which you will pass in a little over half an hour). During 1642 Mayne was one of those Parliamentarians who sat in judgement on Charles I and who signed his death warrant. In 1660, after the restoration of the monarchy, Mayne was condemned to death as a regicide but died in the Tower of London before he could be executed. After this Biggs, his former secretary, became subject to deep melancholy. He became a hermit, living in a shed at Dinton and subsisting on what charity the villagers could spare for him. He kept this up for 36 years, before dying with the secret which was rumoured to have caused his

withdrawal from normal life — that he was one of the masked executioners of the King at Whitehall in January 1643.

Turn left to the cross roads, then right for some 350 yards along the road.

As you cross over the bridge the ford, from which this hamlet apparently got its name, can still be seen on your left.

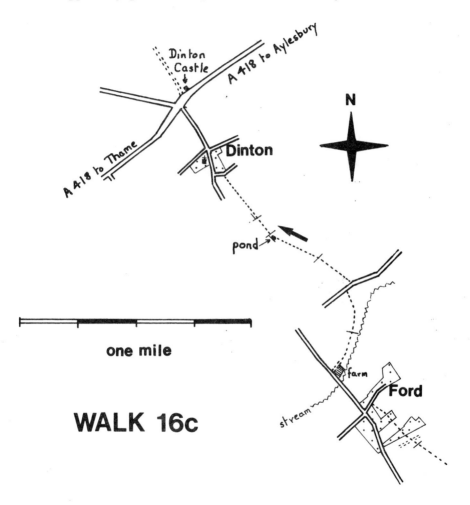

one mile

WALK 16c

Immediately after passing Bridge Farm (on right) turn right along the unmade track between the farm barns and the stone and brick cottage beyond. Go through the gate at the *end* of the track and walk down the middle of the field beyond to leave it by a gate near the centre of the hedge ahead (not visible at first). In the next field, follow an intermittent curving row of bushes in a silted up ditch on your right, skirting the lower end of a fine set of fossilised mediaeval ploughing ridges and furrows.

Coming out on to the Aylesbury–Haddenham road through a gate, turn right for 60 yards, then left over a stile and footbridge into the corner of a field. Head diagonally left across the field, aiming slightly to left of the tower of Dinton church, to go through the hedge ahead* at its mid-point and continue across the following field to its far left-hand corner.

On reaching the corner (it contains a pond) cross the fence in front of you** and, aiming slightly to the right of Dinton Church, go downhill across one field, over a footbridge and stile in the hedge at the bottom and uphill, walking beside the hedge on your left, in the next. When the hedge turns away to left, carry straight on uphill to come out on to the road through a gate in front of the small village school. Turn left to reach a road junction, then right to follow the road uphill for ¼ mile until you come to the Aylesbury–Oxford road (A418) at Dinton Castle.

Dinton parish church has a very fine Norman south doorway. The large house next door to it is Dinton Hall, one-time home of Simon Mayne, who was mentioned at Ford. It is an impressive, but architecturally complex house dating from the fifteenth or sixteenth century.

Cross the A418 and turn right along it for 100 yards.

Dinton Castle Point for joining or leaving the Ring	4¼ miles on to Waddesdon O.S. 1:25,000 scale map SP71 (Pathfinder Series 1093) Our route maps 16d, 16e

Travel

On weekdays Aylesbury Bus service 260 (Aylesbury–Thame), and Oxford Bus services 2 and 280 (Aylesbury–Oxford) combine to give a half-hourly service to Dinton Castle. There is no service on Sundays until late morning, after which Oxford Bus service 2 runs every 2 hours.

Cars can be parked on a broad area of highway verge on the south side of the A418, just west of the crossroads.

---

*In 1988 the stile was missing and it was necessary to detour along the right-hand side of both of these fields, then turn left along the far side of the second to reach its far left-hand corner; a new stile has been requested.
**In 1988 the stile was missing and it was necessary to go a few yards to the left to cross the fence via a horse jump; a new stile has been requested.

Refreshments on the next section

Nothing until you reach Waddesdon which has pubs and village stores. On reaching Waddesdon there is a mobile cafe (usually open daily) and a modern public toilet ¼ mile off the route on a lay-by off the A41 at the east (Aylesbury) end of the village.

Route

"Dinton Castle" is the name given to the roofless stone building standing on a Saxon burial mound in the clump of trees on the north side of the A418. It has a hexagonal ground plan and was built in 1769 by Sir John Vanhattem (of Dinton Hall, a quarter-mile to the south). He intended it partly as an eye-catcher, or folly, partly to display his collection of fossils in its walls, and partly as a summer house.

Go through the gateway on the north side of the A418, 100 yards east (Aylesbury side) of the bus stop lay-by. Immediately inside the gateway take the right forking track past the Castle and on downhill, quickly rejoining the track which had diverged. Follow the track down the right-hand side of the field towards the valley of the River Thame. Keep a sharp lookout for the track's first bend to the right (about 300 yards beyond the Castle). 80 yards after this bend leave the track and cross the horse jump in a gap in the hedge on your right.

As you climb the fence you are facing the truncated end of a hedge dividing the two fields in front of you. Bear left to cross the left-hand field diagonally to its far (bottom) corner, aiming just to the left of the pair of silos seen beyond it. Cross the footbridge* on your left in the corner, and turn right to continue in the next field beside the hedge on your right. In the corner ahead go through the gap in the hedge ahead, over the footbridge* and diagonally left across the next field to its far left-hand corner. Once there, go through the gap in the hedge ahead and on along the left-hand side of the field beyond (now heading straight for the silos) to reach the buildings of Starveall Farm.

Immediately (20 yards) before reaching the farm buildings turn left through the gateway in the hedge and away down the right-hand side of the next two fields, initially skirting along the side of the farm buildings on your right. At the end of the second field go through the gate ahead and strike out diagonally to the right (aiming at 1 o'clock) across the following field to cross the stile and footbridge** in the right-hand boundary (located at the left-hand end of the hedge which forms part of this boundary). Cross the corner of the

*Footbridges missing in 1988 and replacements requested.
**This footbridge has been installed a little to the left of the legal line of the path; it may be resited to its correct position (within the hedge) during the currency of this book.

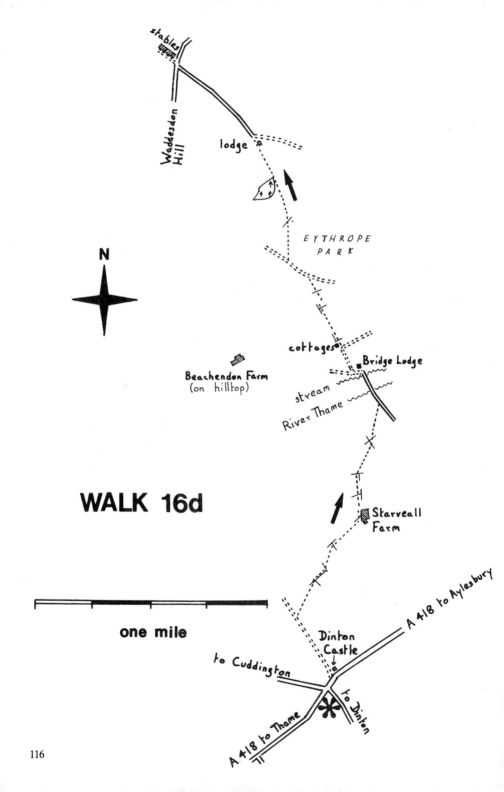

stables

Waddesdon Hill

lodge

N

EYTHROPE PARK

cottages

Bridge Lodge

Beachendon Farm
(on hilltop)

stream

River Thame

WALK 16d

Starveall Farm

one mile

A 418 to Aylesbury

Dinton Castle

to Cuddington

to Dinton

A 418 to Thame

next field, climb the nearby stile in the fence on left, then bear diagonally right across the ensuing field aiming at 2 o'clock to reach a road some 100 yards to the right of the brick parapets of the bridge over the River Thame. To join the road, go over a footbridge in a gap in the hedge. Turn left along the road and follow it over the brick bridge (Eythrope Bridge) and the ensuing bridge over a waterfall.

At the second bridge you enter Eythrope Park, the setting of one of the nineteenth-century houses built in the Vale of Aylesbury by various branches of the Rothschild family of bankers. In this case the owner was Alice de Rothschild and her home, The Pavilion (built 1883), will be seen shortly. The waterfall below the bridge was constructed in the 1880's to raise the level of the River Thame and create an artificial lake as an embellishment of the park.

Follow the estate road as it leaves the bridge and bends sharp left, then sharp right past Bridge Lodge. After a 150-yard straight section (with views on right to The Pavilion, Eythrope Park, partially obscured by trees) the road turns sharp right again. Leave it here on the outside of the bend and maintain your course through the small clump of trees along the side of the pair of cottages. Go through the small gate in the fence ahead into the large, sloping field and maintain your course uphill beside the fence on your left. As you approach the summit cross the stile in the corner ahead and keep beside the fence on your left (now along the side of a young hilltop plantation) as it turns sharp right. When the fence turns left leave it and cross the plantation to go out over the stile in the fence ahead. Then bear left to continue downhill diagonally across the field, passing (in 1988) to right of a mid-field clump of four trees. This course brings you to a stile in the right-hand fence; climb it to join a metalled estate road.

Turn left along the estate road for 150 yards and then leave it through the double gates in the fence on the right. Continue on a farm track across the middle of a gently-rising field. Go through the double gates in the fence ahead and stay on the farm track as it climbs more steeply to pass along the edge of a small wood on the left. At the upper corner of the wood continue straight ahead on the unfenced farm track between fields, to reach the lodge house on the skyline.

The lodge house, with its five-arrow crest (beneath the chimney facing you) representing the five sons of Mayer Amschel Rothschild of Frankfurt (1744–1812) marks the edge of Alice de Rothschild's Eythrope Park.

Go through the gate beside the lodge and straight ahead along the minor road beyond it. Follow the road for half a mile (with panoramic views over

N

A41 to Aylesbury

Waddesdon

school

barns

WALK 16e

stables

one mile

Waddesdon Hill

the Vale of Aylesbury) until it ends at a "T" junction. There cross the road ahead and go through the gates of the Waddesdon Stud Farm.

You are now in the next Rothschild estate — the park surrounding Waddesdon Manor, a hilltop mansion built in the style of a Loire Valley chateau by Baron Ferdinand de Rothschild in 1874–81.

Follow the metalled track past the stables. On reaching the furthest stable block ignore the path sloping down to the left and the white gates into the yard on the right and go straight ahead between them on a narrow path between hedge and fence. Once through the gate ahead continue along the well-trodden path through the belt of trees and climb the stile at the end of it to enter a paddock of the stud farm. Bear left, aiming at 1 o'clock across the paddock to a stile in the hedge ahead (just to right of the far left-hand corner). On the far side of the hedge bear left, immediately cross a second stile into the next paddock and then set off downhill, aiming for the right-hand end of the prominent modern school buildings visible ahead on the outskirts of Waddesdon village. This course quickly brings you to a stile in the fence which curves across your route.

While descending across this paddock, look left to see Waddesdon Manor among the trees on the summit of the next hill to the north-west.

Cross the stile and change direction slightly to right to continue downhill across the next field and leave it via a stile in the bottom fence (seen near the right-hand end of the nearest row of trees). Cross this narrow belt of trees, a farm track and the stile in the fence beyond. Leaving the track squarely behind you cross the corner of the field to the projecting point in the left-hand hedge/fence, some 80 yards ahead. On reaching this point bear slightly left to follow the fence to a stile less than 30 yards on. Climb the stile, pass around the left-hand corner of the garden fence in front of you, and walk downhill, with the fence close on your right to go between farm barns and a house and thereby reach a minor road.

Cross the road obliquely to right to go through a pedestrian gap in the iron fence into a shelter belt of trees. Cross a footbridge just behind the gap and immediately bear right to follow a well-trodden path through the trees to a stile on the edge of the next field.

Cross the field, heading slightly right at 1 o'clock to the stile roughly in the middle of the fence on the skyline ahead. This stile is on the side of a fenced path running between farmland and school playing fields. Turn right along the path towards the nearest houses in Waddesdon and follow it as it turns sharp left in front of a bungalow. Maintain your course when the grass path converges with a tarmac path and, 60 yards after a second kink in the path turn right to cross a stile and walk down a grass path through the middle of the allotments towards the village. At the bottom of the allotments turn right for 15 yards, then turn left to go over a footbridge and along a fenced path to emerge in Baker Street. Turn right along Baker Street, cross over the main A41 road, and continue along the minor road directly opposite.

Waddesdon Point for joining or leaving the Ring	4½ miles on to Hardwick O.S. 1:25,000 scale maps SP71, 81 (Pathfinder Series 1093, 1094) Our route map 16f

Travel

Red Rover services from Aylesbury to Westcott, Edgcott, Steeple Claydon, and Bicester call at Waddesdon on weekdays at roughly hourly intervals; there is no Sunday service on these routes.

Cars can be parked on the broad parking area flanking Waddesdon High Street (A41) at the west end of the village.

Refreshments on the next section

For Waddesdon see start of preceding section; nothing else until Hardwick, which has a pub.

Route

The village of Waddesdon was transformed in appearance and employment prospects by the building of Waddesdon Manor in the 1870's by Baron Ferdinand de Rothschild. For further details see page 22.

Set off along the minor road leaving the north side of the High Street (A41) near the east end of the village; it starts opposite Baker Street and the tyre fitting depot. After 100 yards the access road turns sharp right into a housing estate. At this point take to the fenced/hedged path which maintains your course, skirting the edge of the housing and ending in a field. Bear diagonally right across the field to leave it over a stile in the hedge ahead, 20 yards from the far right-hand corner. On along the right-hand side of the following field, to a stile/footbridge in the right-hand corner ahead.

Leaving the extensive buildings of Glebe Farm away to your left, cross the next field diagonally to the far right-hand corner and leave it through the gateway (which becomes visible at the last moment) in the corner. Now turn sharp left to follow the left-hand hedge until reaching a concrete farm track which crosses your path. Turn right on to the track and follow it towards an isolated group of barns. Some 100 yards before reaching the barns, and immediately after passing below the second of a pair of overhead electricity lines, leave the track through a narrow gap in the left-hand fence (almost opposite the nearest electricity pole to the track). Now maintain roughly your previous course, but diverge slowly from the track to pass over a footbridge in the hedge ahead 50 yards to the left of the barns.

Maintain the same course, diagonally left across the next field aiming at 11 o'clock towards a distant pylon seen in front of a low brick-built farm building. Climb the stile in the hedge ahead and turn left along the road beyond.

The road rises to cross the Aylesbury–Calvert railway line, (formerly the Great Central Railway from London to Sheffield and Manchester). Looking over the bridge parapet on your left you will see the remains of the platforms of Waddesdon station, which closed in 1936. Since this station only opened in 1897 these platforms have stood disused for longer than they were in use.

120

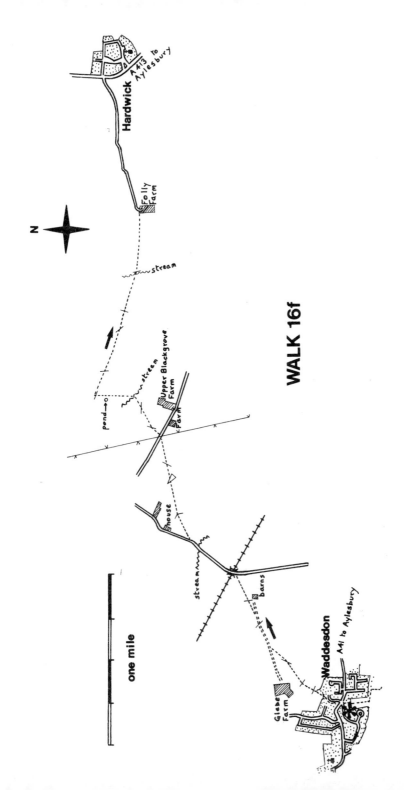

WALK 16f

one mile

N

Hardwick
A 413 to Aylesbury

Folly Farm

stream

stream

pond

Upper Blackgrove Farm

barn

house

stream

Barns

Glebe Farm

Waddesdon
A 41 to Aylesbury

Walk along the road for ¼ mile. Immediately after it crosses a stream and then bends right and left in quick succession leave the road via the footbridge and stile on your right. Cross the sloping field diagonally to left uphill to the highest corner and there go over the stile beside the gate. Change direction *very* slightly right and continue across the following field, now keeping almost on the level and heading just to left of the low group of farm buildings seen ahead beside a pylon. This course brings you to a corner of the field, with a small triangular enclosure protecting a copse of young trees. Cross this enclosure using stiles.

Continue diagonally to right across the corner of the field beyond the copse, to go over the stile in the fence ahead (aiming a little to the right of the lowest point in the nearest span of the pylon line). Maintain the same course diagonally across the ensuing field, to reach a road via a stile and footbridge seen just to the right of the lowest point on the pylon line.

Cross the road, go through the gate opposite, and bear right at 1 o'clock across the corner of the next field for nearly 100 yards to go through the gate in the right-hand hedge/fence. With your back to the gate set your course across the next field diagonally left at 10 o'clock to reach a gate in the middle of the left-hand boundary. (You quickly pass at a right angle beneath an overhead electricity line.) Go through the gate and continue diagonally to right (aiming at 2 o'clock) across the next field to a footbridge over the stream which bounds it.

Once across the stream stop and scan the range of low hills ahead. Pick out Pitchcott, the furthest to left of the villages visible on the skyline. Next locate the church on the skyline at the left-hand end of Pitchcott. Set off across the field aiming straight for the church tower. As you cross the field, leave a small pond 30 yards to your left; it was marked (in 1988) by three trees.

This course brings you to a broad gap in the hedge ahead some 60 yards from the left-hand corner. Go through the gap and immediately turn right to walk beside the hedge on your right along the edge of this field. Go through the gap in the corner ahead and maintain the same direction across the middle of the next three fields going through wide gaps (each with a grassy bridge for tractors) in the hedges between them. In the first field you should be aiming marginally to right of the group of grey farm buildings that you will shortly be passing. While crossing the second field you are heading straight for the farm bungalow beside these buildings. On the far side of the third field go through the gate in the hedge ahead. (The gate is hidden from view until you reach it. In 1988 it was a few trees to right of the highest and biggest of the *clumps* of trees scattered along the hedge; a solitary oak stood in the hedge close to the gate.)

The prominent large red-brick house in the trees on the left-

hand skyline is Oving House, built in the seventeenth century and greatly enlarged a century later.

Bear slightly right uphill across the next field to leave it through a gate in front of the farm bungalow. Once through that gate leave the bungalow on your right and walk along the metalled farm road for ¾ mile to Hardwick. As you leave the farm behind, Hardwick soon becomes visible on the low hill ahead.

Hardwick Point for joining or leaving the Ring	3½ miles on to Rowsham O.S. 1:25,000 scale map SP81 (Pathfinder Series 1094) Our route map 16g

Travel

On weekdays Aylesbury Bus service 66 and Red Rover service 2 (Aylesbury–Winslow–Buckingham) combine to provide roughly an hourly service. There is no Sunday service. Alight at Hardwick bus shelter.

There are no public parking places in Hardwick but it is possible to park a car on street in the village in several places without causing obstruction.

Refreshments on the next section

Hardwick and Weedon have pubs; Weedon has a village store in High Street. Rowsham has no such facilities.

Route

Hardwick, on its hill, stands quietly aside from the hurrying traffic on the A413. In the churchyard, on the south side of the church tower, is a memorial erected in 1818 by Lord Nugent. Beneath it are the bones of 247 humans which had been discovered buried communally near Holman's Bridge, just outside Aylesbury. The bridge is the reputed site of the Battle of Aylesbury, fought in 1642 during the Civil War and in this belief Lord Nugent arranged for the mass of bones to be carried to Hardwick and given a proper burial in consecrated ground. In more recent times research has suggested that the "battle" of Aylesbury was little more than a skirmish, with few casualties. This then leaves the so far unsolved problem of who the 247 were.

Cross the A413 (Aylesbury–Buckingham) road and walk uphill on the road

123

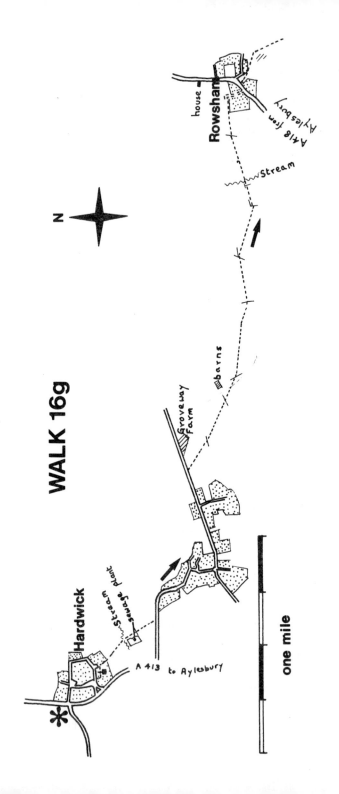

WALK 16g

Rowsham

house

A418 from Aylesbury

Stream

barns

Groveway Farm

Hardwick

Stream

Sewage Plant

A 413 to Aylesbury

N

one mile

into Hardwick. At the top of the hill, by the converted chapel, turn right, leaving the small green on your left. When the road opens out into a second green, take the metalled path along the left-hand side of the grass, cross the road ahead and continue in the same line along a metalled footpath leading between gardens to the church.

Immediately on entering the churchyard turn left and follow the metalled path round two sides of the church (the second side adjoins a farmyard). Just before the end of the second side descend the steps, then resume your course to reach the right-hand corner of the farmyard.

Climb the stile ahead and bear slightly left down into the valley to the rather obtrusive sewer pipe at the corner of the village's small sewage plant. Cross the footbridge over a tributary of the River Thame, followed by a smaller footbridge beside the next corner of the sewage plant. Now follow the right-hand hedge uphill in the next field to go over a stile in the top right-hand corner and out on to a road. Turn left up the road into Weedon and follow its winding course through the village to the crossroads beside the Five Elms public house.

Weedon is well endowed with houses from the seventeenth and eighteenth centuries. One house which you will not see is Lilies, whose boundary wall you skirt on your right as you enter the village. Lilies was built in the early nineteenth century for Lord Nugent and named as a compliment to the heraldic arms of the French Royal Family (it was anticipated that it might become a residence for one of the French Princes who regularly visited the Dukes of Buckingham at Stowe).

Turn left at the crossroads beside the Five Elms public house and follow the Aston Abbotts road out of the village for half a mile from the crossroads. After passing the last house in Weedon continue 200 yards and then, some 160 yards before the buildings of Groveway Farm, turn right over a stile into the corner of the second field beyond the houses.

Bear diagonally left downhill across the field aiming at 11 o'clock to go through the gate found near the middle of the bottom hedge/fence (the gate, which is directly behind the large farm barns is not visible until you are upon it). Maintain the same diagonal course in the next field, soon going uphill and over the ridge ahead to descend the other side and cross the hedge ahead via a stile attached to a tree trunk in the bottom of a dip. Continue on the same course diagonally left downhill across the following field, aiming between 10 and 11 o'clock to go through a gap in the left-hand hedge.

Now change course marginally to right. With your back *squarely* to the hedgerow, aim at 1 o'clock across the huge field which follows, to leave it through a small gate (footbridge missing in 1988) in the hedge ahead. (This gate, which is not visible until you are near, is a little to the right of the distinctive knob of Ivinghoe Beacon, the highest visible point in the Chiltern Hills which run along the horizon; in 1988 it could be located beside the pointing finger of the stump of a solitary dead tree in the hedgerow.)

With the gate squarely behind you, go straight across the next field to go through a field gate in the opposite hedge into the bottom *left*-hand corner of a sloping field. Once through the gate strike uphill diagonally right aiming at 1 o'clock. As you breast the summit your next destination, the hamlet of Rowsham, should be dead ahead.

Continue downhill to cross the stile and footbridge in the nearest section of hedge ahead. (They are seen just to the right of Rowsham and found at the outermost point of this hedge which projects into the field you are in.) From the stile change direction slightly to left and continue downhill in the next field beside the hedge on your left. Climb a stile just before the next corner, and go through a gate/footbridge/stile combination into the left-hand of the two fields ahead. Beyond the stile bear *very* slightly left across the next field to reach the gate near the middle of the hedge ahead. (A cluster of farm barns is visible ahead in the field beyond; the gate itself is in front of the lone barn silhouetted on the near skyline.) On across the next field to go through 3 gates in quick succession and pass beside, then between the barns of Manor Farm; see the paragraph below for notes on these former brewery buildings. Finally turn right along the farm access track to reach the main A418 road which you can hear.

Rowsham Point for joining or leaving the Ring	6 miles on to Aston Clinton O.S. 1:25,000 scale map SP81 (Pathfinder Series 1094) Our route maps 16h, 16i

Travel

Aylesbury Bus services 65, X14, X15 (Reading–High Wycombe–Aylesbury–Leighton Buzzard–Milton Keynes) combine to give a service interval of between 1 and 2 hours to Rowsham on weekdays; on Sundays there is only one bus in the afternoon and one in the evening.

Parking space at Rowsham is very restricted.

Refreshments on the next section

There are no refreshment facilities on this section until you reach the pubs and village shops of Aston Clinton, except for the Rothschild Arms public house at Buckland.

Route

Rowsham, now a hamlet divided by a main road, was once dominated by the brewing industry. As you entered the hamlet you passed one former malthouse and the vaulted remains of a brewery building on your left. There is another former brewery building on the other side of the A418 (just off this walk). The substantial brick house on the inside of the bend on the A418 was built by a nineteenth-century brewer (Joseph Lucas) for himself, and several of the cottages were for brewery workers. Beer production here stopped shortly after 1939.

Turn left along the main road for 60 yards, then cross it and go over the stile beside a farm entrance. Bear diagonally left across the field, and incline further left on rounding the corner of the houses ahead. Go to the stile in the corner just beyond the buildings of Seabrook Farm (on right); cross the stile and footbridge there and, leaving the farm buildings to right, cross the farm track and go through the field gate ahead. Straight up the middle of the field, paralleling the well preserved pattern of mediaeval ridge and furrow ploughing marks, to go over the stile near the middle of the fence/hedge ahead. Straight on again over the summit (leaving a lonely group of farm buildings well to the right) and down to the stile/footbridge 50 yards to left of the gate in the hedge ahead. (The houses of Hulcott are now visible in the trees ahead.) Slightly to right downhill across the next field to cross a prominent footbridge over a headwater of the River Thame.

From the far side of the bridge maintain your previous course, now gently uphill beside the hedge on your right. At the top of the slope the boundary turns away to the right; follow it as it winds past the buildings of a former farm, go through the gate on the right just beyond the farm and continue along the ensuing track on to the village green in Hulcott.

Hulcott is one of the handful of Buckinghamshire parishes with populations numbering less than one hundred persons. Most of the hamlet's houses cluster round the green, but historically its most interesting property is the well preserved moated site behind the church. Although little is known about this particular site, moated sites in general are a mediaeval phenomenon, created in the age-old desire for social advancement. At a time when noblemen were building castles and defending them with moats, lesser men who lacked the authority or capital to fortify their homes, dug moats around them, partly as a defence against roaming animals (and humans?), and partly as a status symbol. The building which

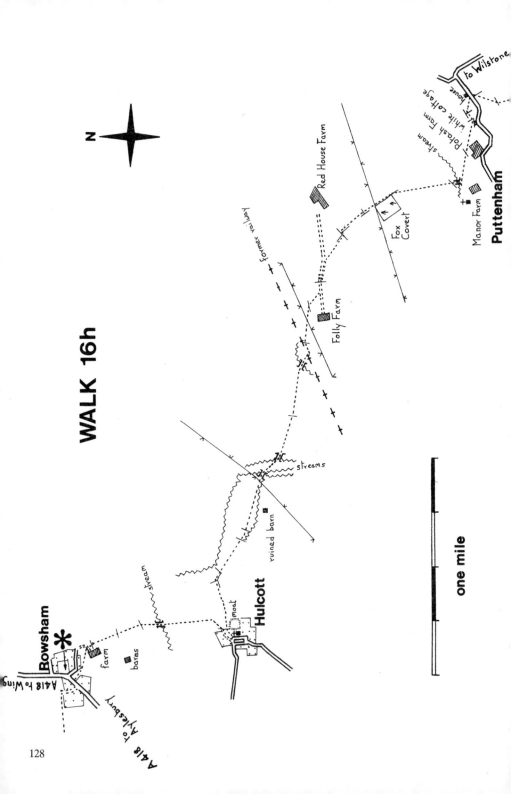

WALK 16h

N

one mile

to Wilstone

Puttenham

Manor Farm

White cottage

Polash Farm

stream

Red House Farm

Fox Covert

Folly Farm

former railway

streams

ruined barn

Hulcott

moat

stream

farm

barns

Bowsham

A418 to Wing

A418 to Aylesbury

128

once stood on the island vanished long ago, but the moated site passed at Denham on Walk No. 11 is still occupied.

The next four miles are across an almost flat outcrop of Gault Clay, over which several headstreams of the River Thame wind slowly. It is an area with a special character which gradually dominates you. It is almost without roads or villages and, after leaving Hulcott, traffic noise fades away, bird and animal sounds become more prominent, and you feel that you are intruding in a private world. It is remarkably lonely for an area so close to Aylesbury.

No sooner have you reached the main part of the green than you must turn left off it, through the next gate in the hedge on the left (i.e. *before* reaching the churchyard wall). Aim very slightly to left across the small paddock to climb the stile ahead. Beyond the stile (you may recognise the field!) bear slightly right to walk alongside one arm of Hulcott's moated site. At the next corner of the moat leave it and continue straight ahead beside the fence/ditch on your right. Cross the stile/footbridge ahead in the field corner and turn right along a raised grassy causeway to go through the gate 70 yards away. Maintain the same course along the causeway winding across the next field (a hedge slowly converges from the right) to reach the gate and tractor bridge seen 25 yards to left of the next field corner.

The low earthworks immediately on your right are probably the remains of a complex set of artificial fishponds, built during the mediaeval period to give somebody (possibly the occupier of the moated house?) a regular supply of food. A series of hand-dug channels would have taken the water from the moat through the various fishtanks and on down to the stream on your left. Once the system became disused it would rapidly have silted up. The bank on which you are walking was probably the dyke which held water into the system.

Once across the bridge bear slightly right across the corner of the next field to go through the gate in the next corner ahead. Then bear left, aiming at between 10 and 11 o'clock across this irregularly shaped field to pass close by the right-hand side of the pylon in this field and continue into the field corner. Once there, go over a brick bridge which spans a confluence of streams and a county boundary. Beyond the bridge bear at 1 o'clock across the first field in Hertfordshire to cross the farm access bridge over the stream ahead.

With the stream squarely behind you bear very slightly right (uphill at first) across the next two fields (with a gate in the fence between them), heading between 12 and 1 o'clock towards the farmhouse and barns of Folly Farm, which are seen in a gap in the hedge ahead. At the far side of the second field cross the farm access bridge over the stream, and continue through the small paddock beyond to pass through the substantial double hedge line ahead via a pair of gates.

The double hedge encloses the shallow earthworks of the former Cheddington–Aylesbury branch railway and you are on a one-time level crossing. Opened in 1839 as a feeder to the Euston–Birmingham main line, this was one of the earliest branch lines in Britain. It was eclipsed when the Metropolitan Railway built a more direct route from London to Aylesbury in 1892 and finally closed to passengers in 1953 — one of the earliest branches to lose its passenger service.

Once over the level crossing turn sharp left to walk beside the former railway and cross the stiles and footbridge in the field corner. Then leave the railway and go diagonally to right across the next field to pass beneath the overhead electricity line midway between the two nearest pylons. Go through the second gate in the right-hand hedge (just beyond the paddock beside the farmhouse) and continue diagonally left across the next field to cross the stile in the opposite hedge midway between two poles of an overhead electricity line.

Turn left along the track from Folly Farm for 60 yards. Immediately after the track has passed through a hedgerow, go through the gateway into the field on right, then resume your course along the curving left-hand edge of this field to reach the next right-angled field corner. Cross the horse jump ahead of you in the corner, turn sharp left to the next field corner (only a few paces) and go through the gap in the hedge in front of you. Now turn right to walk beside this hedge along the edge of the field.

As you follow the hedge you are crossing the ends of a fine series of fossilised mediaeval ploughing marks. Preservation to this standard implies that this field has not been ploughed since the open field system of cultivation (see page 93) was ended here.

Go through the gate in the corner ahead and on along the right-hand side of the following field. (The houses away to the left are at Long Marston.) You soon pass along the side of a small wood and, on reaching the far end of it, cross the stile in the right-hand fence into a field across which Puttenham church can be seen. Aim across the field to the left-hand end of the group of buildings (Manor Farm) standing amidst trees to the left of the church (ignore the farm with two silo towers standing further to left). As you come over the shallow rise in the field, a stile and footbridge appear in the hedge ahead; go over them and bear right across the narrow paddock beyond to cross a footbridge over a drainage channel.

The tiny hamlet of Puttenham has the distinction of being the westernmost settlement in Hertfordshire. Note the attractive flint chequerwork on the church's nave and tower — evidence that the chalk and flints of the Chiltern Hills are near enough for these materials to have been carried here in the fourteenth and fifteenth centuries when the church was built.

Once across the bridge bear diagonally left across the field to leave it through the gate at the left-hand corner of the buildings of Potash Farm with its dominant silo towers; maintain the same course across the next field to reach the pair of white-painted cottages. In the field corner just to the left of the cottages go over a small brick bridge into a fenced path. Climb the stile ahead and go diagonally right across the ensuing field to the far right-hand corner (just to right of the house) to reach the Puttenham–Astrope road.

Cross the road, go over the stile diagonally opposite, and the stile immediately beyond that, then turn sharp right over a horse jump into the adjoining field. Cross that field diagonally to left and go through the gate in the far left-hand corner. Continue in the next field beside the hedge on your right and stay with the hedge when it turns to the right. At the next field corner go over the stiles and footbridge ahead and (now back in Buckinghamshire) continue along the right-hand side of the following field to reach a gate on to the road near Puttenham Lock. Turn left along the road to go over the canal bridge at the lock.

The Aylesbury branch canal leaves the London–Birmingham Grand Union Canal and drops down through no less than 16 locks to terminate at Aylesbury. With so many locks to climb every time a boat leaves Aylesbury, it would not have been surprising if this branch had fallen into disuse when freight carrying on the canal ended in 1964. Today, however, Aylesbury basin is a thriving base for canal touring boats and, during the summer, you are quite likely to see one at Puttenham Lock working to or from Aylesbury.

Quickly leave the road by turning right into the field over the footbridge beside the first gate beyond the canal bridge. Then turn left to skirt the left-hand field boundary for some 220 yards before crossing a stile and footbridge in the left-hand boundary. (As an added check count the sharp turns in the side of this irregularly shaped field; after the third turn in quick succession continue for 60 yards to find the stile and footbridge.)

With the footbridge squarely behind you cross the next field diagonally to the right (aiming at 1 o'clock) to cross a stile and footbridge in the opposite hedge. Once across the footbridge turn right and follow the ditch as it snakes along the sinuous right-hand edge of this field. Ignore side gates and

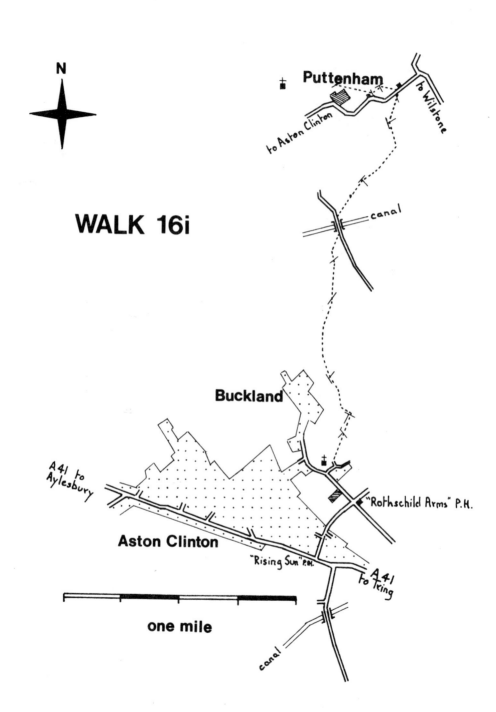

N

WALK 16i

Puttenham

to Aston Clinton

to Wilstone

canal

Buckland

A41 to Aylesbury

"Rothschild Arms" P.H.

Aston Clinton

"Rising Sun" P.H.

A41 to Tring

canal

one mile

persevere until you come to an actual *corner of this field*. At that point go over the stile ahead and continue along the right-hand edge of the next field (the houses of Buckland are now visible one field away to the right). Soon the field boundary makes a pronounced turn to the left; 100 yards beyond this point turn right over the stile and footbridge and cross the right-hand end of the adjoining field to climb the stile in the opposite hedge. Now, with Buckland church visible ahead, go diagonally to the far left-hand corner of the following paddock and out through the gate there. Follow the short grassy lane on the outskirts of Buckland for a few yards until it reaches a village road opposite Manor Farm.

> **Buckland is another of the long, narrow parishes running up the Chiltern escarpment — we saw another one earlier on The Ring at Kimble. At Buckland the parish is only ½ mile wide in the vicinity of the village, but it extends for over 5 miles from north to south up into the Chilterns. In the latter part of the nineteenth century the parish was dominated by its vicar, the Rev. Edward Bonus, who lived there for 50 years until his death in 1908. No services were held in the parish church when he was absent on visits to the Holy Land, but when in residence he *ordered* his parishioners to attend evensong. Perhaps the fact that he owned a number of the cottages in the village had something to do with his rather authoritarian approach to his flock!**

Turn right along the road, left at the road junction, and right at the crossroads by the Rothschild Arms public house to follow the pavement of the Lower Icknield Way (B489) into Aston Clinton. The road ends at a junction with the A41 (London–Aylesbury) road beside the Rising Sun public house at the east end of the village of Aston Clinton.

Aston Clinton Point for joining or leaving the Ring	3½ miles on to Wendover O.S. 1:25,000 scale maps SP80, 81 (Pathfinder Series 1094, 1118) Our route map 16j

Travel

Aston Clinton is served on weekdays by roughly 4 buses per hour on a variety of routes of which the principal ones are Aylesbury Bus/Red Rover 61 (Aylesbury–Tring–Luton), London Country Northwest 501 (Aylesbury–Tring–Watford), and Greenline 768 (Aylesbury–Tring–London). On Sundays frequency is down to one or two per hour, and London Country route 501 and

Greenline 768 are replaced by Marshalls 501 (Aylesbury–Hemel Hempstead–Watford). Alight at The Rising Sun, Aston Clinton (at the east end of the village).

Refreshments on the next section

There are pubs in Aston Clinton (The Rising Sun is actually on the route; The Bell Inn has an international reputation and is a little up-market if you are dressed for walking!). Aston Clinton also has a supermarket on the main road through the village, about a quarter-mile west of The Rising Sun. Halton has no facilities, but Wendover has a number of pubs and shops, including cafes.

Route

Turn left along the A41 for 100 yards from The Rising Sun, then first right up Stable Bridge Road. After a further 300 yards you reach a narrow canal bridge guarded by traffic lights. Immediately beyond it turn right off the road and drop down to join the canal towpath. Turn left, and set off along the towpath with the canal on your *right*. Stay on the towpath for 3 miles to Wendover.

The Wendover Arm of the Grand Union Canal was completed in 1797, its main purpose being to supply water from springs above Wendover to the summit level of the Grand Union near Tring. By 1802 it was noticed that the Wendover Arm was leaking and, in spite of various attempts to seal the problem section (from Drayton Beauchamp to Little Tring), by 1894 the Arm was leaking so badly that it was drawing water off the main line instead of feeding it. The Wendover Arm was closed to canal traffic between Tring and Wendover in 1897 (one of the earliest canal closures in the country) and in 1904 its water was transferred to pipes beneath the leaking section, and the water level of the remainder of the arm was lowered to what you see today. The clear spring water which you see flowing along the bottom of the one-time canal still feeds the main line of the canal at Tring.

About one mile after you joined the towpath you pass between the playing fields and airfield of RAF Halton, home of the Air Force's No. 1 School of Technical Training since 1922. Although the trainees get flying experience in gliders here, the aircraft usually seen parked near the hangars on your right are permanent fixtures for training purposes and unlikely ever to take off again.

Late in 1988 the Government announced that the School

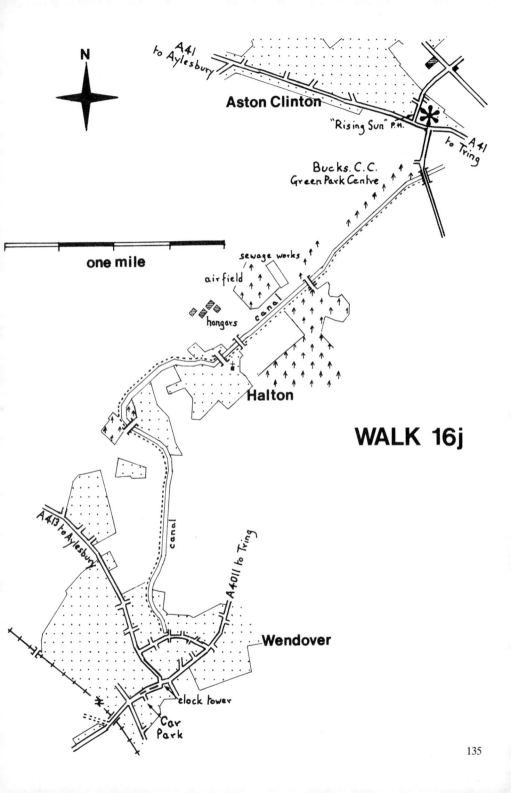

N

A41 to Aylesbury

Aston Clinton

"Rising Sun" P.H.

A41 to Tring

Bucks. C.C.
Green Park Centre

one mile

sewage works

airfield

canal

hangars

Halton

WALK 16j

A413 to Aylesbury

canal

A4011 to Tring

Wendover

clock tower

Car Park

of Technical Training is to be moved to RAF Cosford, in Warwickshire, between 1989 and 1995. The RAF presence at Halton will be heavily reduced and the scene at which you are looking may thus change quite noticeably during these years. The RAF has been an integral part of the life of nearby Wendover for so long that the change will take some getting used to.

The towpath changes from the left to the right side of the canal at the concrete bridge in the village of Halton.

The canal ends at the Town Basin, Wendover, with Wharf Road running across the head of the Basin and the water feeder culvert coming in beneath the road. Note the brick-faced wharf on your left (the wharf itself is now a sloping garden) and the small brick buildings on it which once served the canal company.

On reaching the end of the canal turn right in the road running across the head of the Basin (Wharf Road) and follow it to its junction with the A413 (Amersham–Aylesbury) road; there turn left to reach Wendover Clock Tower. If this is the end of your walk you can catch a bus back to Aylesbury from here. If not, turn right at the Clock Tower to walk up to the top of the High Street. To continue the route description turn back to the beginning of this chapter.

Footpath Publications
from
Buckinghamshire County Council

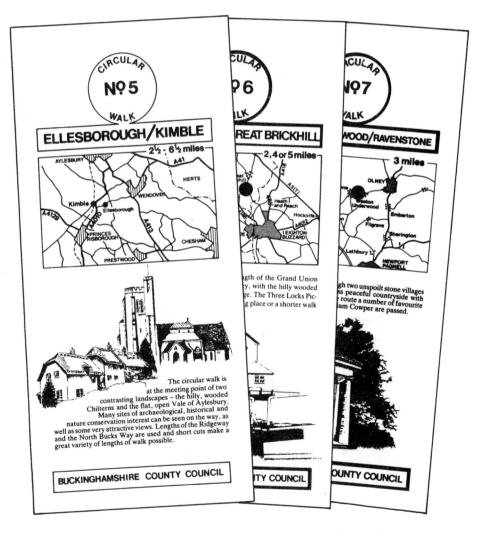

CIRCULAR **No 5** WALK

ELLESBOROUGH/KIMBLE

2½ - 6½ miles

AYLESBURY
A41
HERTS
Kimble
WENDOVER
Ellesborough
A4129
A413
PRINCES RISBOROUGH
CHESHAM
PRESTWOOD

The circular walk is at the meeting point of two contrasting landscapes – the hilly, wooded Chilterns and the flat, open Vale of Aylesbury. Many sites of archaeological, historical and nature conservation interest can be seen on the way, as well as some very attractive views. Lengths of the Ridgeway and the North Bucks Way are used and short cuts make a great variety of lengths of walk possible.

BUCKINGHAMSHIRE COUNTY COUNCIL

CULAR **6** LK

REAT BRICKHILL

2, 4 or 5 miles

Heath and Reach
A5
Hockliffe
LEIGHTON BUZZARD

gth of the Grand Union y, with the hilly wooded ge. The Three Locks Pic-g place or a shorter walk

TY COUNCIL

CULAR **No 7** ALK

WOOD/RAVENSTONE

3 miles

OLNEY
Weston Underwood
Emberton
Filgrave
Sherington
Lathbury
NEWPORT PAGNELL

gh two unspoilt stone villages ss peaceful countryside with route a number of favourite am Cowper are passed.

OUNTY COUNCIL

137

Circular walks

The County Council promotes a series of circular walks in Buckinghamshire. Free illustrated leaflets are available describing the routes and giving background information about things that can be seen on the walks. "Circular Walk" waymarks identify the routes through the countryside, making them easy to follow. Most walks are between 3 and 6 miles and many offer the option of a short cut.

1. **North Marston/Oving** A 5-mile route mainly on bridleways, starting from the historic village of North Marston. Part of the route is along an ancient path once used by pilgrims.

2. **Thornborough** Starting from the mediaeval bridge, this 4½-mile walk passes beside the old Buckingham Arm of the Grand Union Canal, part of which is now a nature reserve. Both the Great Ouse and Padbury Brook are crossed and associated wildlife can easily be seen.

3. **Cuddington/Upper Winchendon** This walk has views of Waddesdon Manor and provides undulating walking along the River Thame Valley. It is 4½ miles long or 3 miles using the short cut.

4. **Brill/Boarstall** The Brill area has many historic sites including the Windmill and Common, parts of the ancient Forest of Bernwood and Boarstall Duck Decoy. These can all be seen on this 4½-mile circular walk.

5. **Ellesborough/Kimble** The circular walk is at the meeting point of two contrasting landscapes — the hilly, wooded Chilterns and the flat, open Vale of Aylesbury. Good views and many sites of historical, archaeological and nature conservation interest can be seen. There is a choice of walks between 2½ and 6½ miles.

6. **Three Locks/Great Brickhill** A length of the Grand Union Canal towpath combined with the hilly wooded countryside of the Greensand Ridge make an interesting walk with plenty of views. There are choices of walks between 2½ and 6 miles.

7. **Weston Underwood/Ravenstone**   This 3-mile walk passes through two unspoilt stone villages and in between the paths cross peaceful countryside with some panoramic views.

8. **Hambleden/Medmenham**   A combination of Chiltern woodlands, the Thames towpath, the Hamble Valley and two pretty villages make this an interesting and varied walk. There is a choice of walks between 2½ and 5½ miles.

9. **Stewkley**   Historic Stewkley is the starting place for this 5-mile circular walk, which passes through attractive peaceful countryside. The walk uses an old Roman road and a sheep-drovers' track on the route.

Linear and long-distance walks

Illustrated leaflets are also produced describing linear and long-distance walks in the county.

1. **North Bucks Way**   This 33-mile long distance path was set up by the Ramblers' Association in 1972 and updated by Buckinghamshire County Council in 1988. It runs from the Chilterns to the county boundary near Milton Keynes, where it joins the Grafton Way.

2. **Two Ridges Link**   This 8-mile linear walk connects two long-distance footpaths — the Ridgeway at Ivinghoe Beacon with the Greensand Ridge Walk at Leighton Buzzard.

3. **Chess Valley Walk**   The walk follows the Chess Valley between Chesham and Rickmansworth. It is 11 miles long and has two connecting paths to nearby stations for anyone not wishing to walk the full length.

Further information   The series of walks is being added to continually. Please contact the Recreational Paths Officer for up-to-date information or with ideas for possible waymarked walks.

BUCKINGHAMSHIRE COUNTY COUNCIL

Rights of Way leaflet

A leaflet explaining rights and responsibilities concerning public paths is available, free of charge, from the County Council. It aims to help walkers, landowners, Parish Councils and all who use and care for the countryside.

Definitive Map

The route of each public right of way is recorded on the Definitive Map, which is under constant review by the County Council. Map sheets are available for inspection at County Hall or at District Council offices. Relevant copies are supplied to Parish Councils.

Leaflets For copies of leaflets, please send SAE to:
Recreational Paths Officer
Engineer's Department
Buckinghamshire County Council
County Hall
Aylesbury
Bucks HP20 1UY
or phone Aylesbury (0296) 382845